MW01698041

WRESTLING

Price Guide

Figures Edition
Volume 1

OVER 450 PICTURES

WRESTLING PRICE GUIDE FIGURES EDITION VOLUME 1

Martin S. Burris

Copyright © 2018 Martin S. Burris and Wrestling Price Guides ISBN Number 978-1-7770751-0-1

All rights reserved.

No part of this publication may be reproduced in any form or by any means, including scanning, photocopying, or otherwise without prior written permission of the copyright holder.

The author has tried to be an authentic source of the information provided in this book. However, the author does not oppose the additional information available over the internet in an updated form.

While all attempts have been made to verify information provided in this publication, the Author assumes no responsibility for errors, omissions, or contrary interpretation of the subject matter herein. Any perceived slights of specific people or organizations are unintentional.

Ebook formatting by www.ebooklaunch.com

Contents

Original San Francisco Toy Makers
Just Toys 'Bend-Ems'
Playmates Toy Company Guide
Galoob WCW Figures
Toy Biz WCW
New Japan Pro Wrestling

Introduction

Few would argue that wrestling fans are one of the most fanatical sports fanbases around. Contrary to popular belief, the wrestling fanbase isn't limited to the WWE rather it stretches to the WWF, NWA, AWA, WCW, NJPW, and UFC. Today, wrestling is followed by millions, if not billions, of people around the world.

Wrestling collectibles such as wrestling cards, figures and memorabilia are a major reason professional wrestling has so many fans. Wrestling figures were among the favorite toys of kids in the 80s and 90s. Many of those kids have maintained their passion for wrestling figures to date even though they're all grown up now.

If you're among the above, then I'm betting that you go out of your way to find your favorite wrestling figures. Fortunately for you, wrestling figures and other wrestling collectibles are easily available and at affordable prices. However, to get the best deal, you must find out how much each wrestling figure/set is worth.

Yes, you have a love for wrestling but that does not mean that you should throw money down the drain. Don't pay hundreds for something that costs less than $20. Most wrestling fans are guilty of doing this.

Wrestling fans are extremely passionate about wrestling. They want to buy every wrestling figure and every version of it and why not: some wrestling figures are worth hundreds of dollars. Most collectors know who has that rare figure and also if that rare figure is just urban legend and doesn't exist.

While collecting wrestling figures is fun, there are some cons to it. For instance, the aftermarket of pro wrestling figures isn't as organized as some of the other toy franchises such as Barbie and Star Wars. Tracking value of professional wrestling figures is quite hard as there is no official price guide bible. So, how do you know if a wrestling figure or other collectible is worth a fortune? This is a problem that we hope to solve.

After you've read this book or wrestling price guide, you'll know what wrestling collectibles are available and what their price is. This will ensure that you don't buy a wrestling collectible for more than what it's worth. Additionally, this will help you to get the best possible deal for a collectible you own.

An overview of wrestling figures

It wouldn't be wrong to say that wrestling figures have fed our obsession with pro wrestling. Today, we're avid wrestling fans only because of these toys. Wrestling figures first became popular in the 1980s. This was the time when the World Wrestling Entertainment, known as World Wrestling Federation then, first came to the fore.

In the 1980s, WWE characters such as Rowdy Roddy piper and Hulk Hogan made the headlines each day. Seeing the popularity of these characters, a company called LJN decided to produce rubber figures that resembled the WWE stars. Since then, many companies have followed suit. Some of the popular wrestling figure manufacturers include Jakks Pacific, Hasbro, and Mattel.

After 1989, LJN stopped producing wrestling figures. However, other toy manufacturers took over the responsibility and are producing the figures even today. Wrestling figures are relatively young in the marketplace when you compare them to other popular collectibles such as Barbie and GI Joe.

In their early days, wrestling figures were quite primitive. They had a rubber molding and were made of wire skeletons. Fortunately, they evolved over time: First into plastic dolls with bendable joints and then into stretchable figures. LJN gets the credit for the 8-inch figures, the thumb wrestlers, the stretch wrestlers, and the bendies while Hasbro was the one that introduced the small, three-inch figures with movable parts.

By mid 1990s, the wrestling figure industry was well established. Seeing this, Jakks Pacific entered the industry and produced 6-inch figures. Compared to the wrestling figures of LJN and Hasbro, Jakks Pacific's figures came with more movement, costumes, and designs. Today, the majority of the aforementioned figures are collectibles.

Many of the wrestling figures produced in the 80s and 90s came with a biography card of the wrestler called a wrestling card. Figures that came with a wrestling card had a higher price than those without it. This is something we'll discuss in detail in the wrestling cards section.

Coming back to the wrestling figures, choices are a plenty in the wrestling figure market as wrestling figures comes in different materials and sizes. Also, you'll find both licensed and unlicensed wrestling figures. Before you buy wrestling figures for yourself, you must determine what you want them for i.e. for the fun of play or developing a collection.

The best wrestling figures will depend on what you want the wrestling figures for. If you're a collector then the first thing that you need to decide is whether you want licensed or unlicensed wrestling figures.

Created with higher quality materials, licensed figures are generally more expensive and hold more value. If you're someone who follows wrestling with a passion and knows both the wrestling personalities of the past and the present then deciding which figures to collect won't be a problem for you. With the aforementioned knowledge, you will be able to better organize your wrestling figure collection.

To find a wrestling figure with a high worth, look at the current prices of all the wrestling figures available in the market.

Most of the earliest wrestling figures were bought solely as toys for children to play with. Back then, there was hardly any concept of preserving the wrestling figures as collectibles. This is one the reasons finding 60s and 70s wrestling figures in good condition is hard.

If you do find a 60s or 70s wrestling figure in a good condition, it is probably going to be worth hundreds of dollars. Nonetheless, to find out how much a 60s or 70s wrestling figure will cost you, you should take a look at a price list of 60s and 70s wrestling figures.

One of the best ways to determine the worth of a wrestling figure is to look at its condition. Wrestling figures available in a packaging will be worth more than those taken out of it. However, a figure without a packaging will have considerable value if it is well maintained. Also, the price of a packaged wrestling figure will vary based on the condition of the packaging.

The good thing is that there are websites that can help you to determine the value of every wrestling figure produced since the 1960s. How do they do that? Simple, by providing you a wrestling price guide. Since this book is a wrestling price guide, you'll be in a good position to determine which wrestling figures to buy and which ones to avoid once you've finished reading this book. To get you started, following are a few recommendations.

If you're a series collector then the WWE Classic Superstar collection would be a good choice for you. Produced in the 2000s, the WWE Classic Superstar collection was developed by Jakks Pacific. These wrestling figures by Jakks Pacific hold more value than the classics of 80s and 90s simply because of their collection and detail aspect.

In this series, you'll find figures of wrestling legends such as The Ultimate Warrior, Ric Flair, and The Undertaker. The WWE Classic Superstar collection contains fifteen different series with each series boasting a minimum of 8 figures.

Another useful suggestion is that you should buy collections released with American cards rather than buying those issued with foreign cards.

The reason for this is simple: collections issued with Americans cards are worth a lot more than collections released with foreign cards.

So, there you have it—an overview of wrestling figures including a brief history of their production since the 1980s and what wrestling figures are best as collectibles. With that over and done with, it's time to take a look at some of the legendary action/wrestling figures of the 60s, the 70s, the 80s, the 90s, and the 2000s. The information on the wrestling figures of the 80s, 90s, and 2000s will help you to do two things: find out the price of the different wrestling figures produced since the 1960s and determine which wrestling figures are worth buying.

Figures 60s

If you think that the wrestling figures produced by LJN in the 1980s were the first ever action figures to hit the market then you're a 100% wrong. Contrary to what you believe, action figures existed long before LJN gave us wrestling figures to play with and collect.

Toys for boys, action figures first hit the toy market in the 1960s. During the early part of the 60s, Hasbro, an American toy and board game company, thought about introducing a 'doll' for boys. Since the company was aware that the idea of playing with dolls wouldn't appeal to boys, Hasbro named its doll 'GI Joe' and marketed it as an 'action figure'. This is how the first action figure was born.

The 1940s film "The Story of G .I. Joe" inspired the name of the G .I. Joe action figure. The G .I. Joe action figure was loved and adored by the children of the 60s. A major reason for this was that the figure helped the kids of the 60s to emotionally connect with members of their family who had served in World War 2 as soldiers, pilots, and sailors.

The G.I Joe action figure was a way for the boys of the 60s to become part of the missions and battle their fathers, grandfathers and uncles were a part of.

The G.I Joe action figure was designed to serve the same purpose that Barbie did for girls. Created by Stan Weston and Don Levine, toy designers at Hasbro, the first G.I. Joe action figure was released in four different boxes. Each box had a G.I. Joe action figure representing a different branch of the military.

The released G.I. Joe action figures include the Action Pilot, Action Marine, Action Sailor, and Action Marine. Each figure came with a duty cap and its basic fatigues. The best thing about this action figure line was that you could buy different military clothing and accessory to festoon your figures into different military looks.

Each G.I. Joe figure had a scar on its right cheek. This was one of its most noticeable features. You may think this feature was a way to attract the kids but the reality is a bit different. The purpose of having a scar on the right cheek of the G.I. Joe figure was to prevent other toy companies from copying the toy design.

1960s was a time when military fervor was at its highest. Due to this reason, small plastic soldiers and fake guns became a huge with kids and even some adults. Quite simply, the new action figure of Hasbro had struck a chord.

The G.I. Joe action figure of Hasbro spurred more toy companies into action and it wasn't long before other 'action figures' started to enter the toy market.

The Astronauts and aliens of Mattel

The first to imitate Hasbro was Mattel, an American toy manufacturing company established in 1945. Major Matt Mason was the name Mattel gave to its action figures. The figures introduced by Mattel were astronauts and the design of most of these figures was inspired by actual NASA prototypes.

Though both of them were action figures, G.I. Joe and Major Matt Mason had quite a few differences. First of all, unlike the G.I. Joe figure of Hasbro, the Major Matt Mason figures of Mattel did not feature any hinge style joints. Instead, they had a runner suited body and a wire inner frame. Moreover, the Major Matt Mason figures were much smaller than the G.I. Joe action figures.

In terms of design and durability, the Major Matt Mason action figure of Mattel was a bit of a hit and miss. However, it was good enough for the era during which it was released.

The astronaut figures and the alien released later were the stars of the Major Matt Mason action figure series. However, the amazing playsets and vehicles that came with the figures were what really caught the eye. Ultimately, the playsets and vehicles became the life-blood or heart of the line.

The Major Matt Mason action figure line rose to popularity almost immediately after its launch. However, the popularity was short-lived. After being adored all through the 60s, the Major Matt Mason action figure line lost its charm during the early part of the 70's as the interest in real-life space adventures started to dissipate.

Nonetheless, those who played with it during the 60s still fondly remember the Major Matt Mason action figure line. In fact, they're always on the lookout for Major Matt Mason astronauts and alien figures in good condition.

Ideal's Captain Action

As mentioned earlier, the 60s was an era in which a flurry of action figures entered the toy market. One of them was the Captain Action figure of Ideal, an American toy company most famous for introducing the Rubik's Cube.

Coming back to the subject at hand, seeing the success of the G.I. Joe action figure, Ideal decided during the latter part of 1965 to launch an action figure of its own. The decision was taken after Stan Weston, the toy designer who designed the popular G. I. Joe figure, took the concept of a single hero that could turn into several super heroes to the company.

In 1966, Ideal launched Captain Action, a figure with a wardrobe of costumes that allowed him to become many different super heroes including Captain America, Superman, Spider man, the Green Hornet, Flash, the Phantom, Aquaman, and Fury.

Captain Action was a 12" figure and came with a sword, gun, and hat in addition to the aforementioned costumes. Available throughout the United States, the Captain Action figure line came with a Villain called Dr. Evil.

Not long after its launch, the Captain Action figure became a hit with kids. Seeing the success of its action figure, Ideal introduced a sidekick called Action Boy. Just like the protagonist, the sidekick came with an array of costumes to don.

The success of the Captain Action figure line propelled Ideal to release a companion line called Super Queens, an action figure line meant for girls. The Super Queens figure line of Ideal included four heroines: Wonder Woman, Supergirl, Mera, and Batgirl. Unlike the Captain Action figure, the Super Queens figure line did not come with any costumes so the figures in the Super Queens figure line stayed as they were.

While the Captain Action figure rose to popularity almost immediately after its launch, it was unable to sustain the success for too long. Only a few years after it was launched, the sales of the Captain Action figure started to decline and it wasn't long before the line was discontinued.

Being specific, the Captain Action figure line lasted for about 2 .5 years. The life span of the Super Queens figure line was even shorter. For this reason, the boxed Captain Action and Super Queens figures feature among the rarest action figures in history. If you own a boxed Captain Action or a Super Queen figure then believe me, you stand to earn a fortune.

The alien figures of Colorforms

Unlike Ideal, Colorforms did not take inspiration for its action figures from Hasbro's G.I. Joe. Instead, Colorforms entered the toy market with action figures of its own after seeing the success of Mattel's Major Matt Mason line.

Seeing the success of the action figures for boys such as G.I. Joe and Major Matt Mason, Colorforms, an American toy manufacturing company, decided to enter the action figure market. The company wanted to create a line that could be used in unison with the Mason line of Mattel. In 1968, Colorforms launched the Outer Space Men figure line, a line featuring alien figures with a bendable wire frame and a rubber body.

The Outer Space Men figure line included 3.5" to 7" alien figures. Each alien belonged to a different planet, something obvious from their name. Some of the figures in the Outer Space Men figure line were "Alpha 7, the Man from Mars" and "Colossus Rex, the Man from Jupiter."

The figures became a major hit almost immediately after their launch but like most other action figures of the 60s, they failed to sustain their success. The first series of the Outer Space Men figure line was its last one.

Just like the Captain Action and Super Queen figures of Ideal, the Outer Space Men figures of Colorforms are among the rarest action figures in history. This means that if own an Outer Space Men figure today, you can get good money for it.

The action figures of the 60s set the tone for the rest to follow. It was the figures of the 60s that inspired the one-man- army figures of the 70s and the wrestling figures of the 80s, which later inspired the wrestling figures of the 90s and 2000s. In short, there wouldn't have been any Han solo, Obi-Wan Kenobi, the six million dollar man, Hulk Hogan or Bret the Hitman Hart figures if Hasbro hadn't taken the initiative to launch the G.I. Joe action figure. The next era of action figures that we're going to look at is the 70s.

Figures 70s

Are you a Millenial or part of the Generation Z? If yes then '**That '70s Show**' is probably the first thing that spring to your mind when someone mentions the 70s era to you. However, there is so much more to the 70s than just the television show mentioned above.

70s was a good time. People listened to different genres of music, wore hippie dresses, and watched TV shows such as the Six Million Dollar Man and Kojak. Moreover, 70s was when the Stars Wars first came into our lives.

Regardless of when you were born, if you're a Star Wars fan then the 70s has to have a special place in your life. You cannot be a true Star Wars fan if you don't acknowledge the importance of the 70s. In addition to the aforementioned things, 70s was a time when a lot of experimentation was done with action figures.

During the 70s, action figures of all sorts including one-man-army figures, alien figures, superhero figures, and sci-fi figures were launched with immense fervor. This is something the Generation X kids will remember well.

Some of the 60s action figures such as G.I. Joe still existed in the 70s. While it was still being sold in the 70s, the G.I. Joe action was re-marketed as 'the Adventure Team'. Unlike the G. I. Joe action figure of the 60s, the 70s G. I. Joe action figure was an all-purpose adventurer who wrestled a giant and raided tombs of mummies.

70s was a time when the martial arts craze was at its highest. Seeing this, Hasbro launched a martial arts version of the G. I. Joe action figure called 'Kung Fu Grip'. This version of G .I. Joe was made out of a softer plastic which enabled the figure to grip objects, hence the name: 'Kung Fu Grip'. Not long after it was first launched, the Kung Fu Grip version of the G. I. Joe action figure was modified with a lever in the back of its head which allowed it to have an 'eagle eye vision'.

The superheroes of Mego

There was resurgence in the popularity of superheroes in the 1970s. Most of the credit for this goes to the superhero figures launched by Mego, an American toy company established in 1954.

The World's Greatest Superheroes was the name Mego gave to its superhero figure line. After obtaining the licensing rights for most of the Marvel and DC characters, Mego launched its superhero figure line for the first time in 1972. The first version of the World's Greatest Superheroes included 8" action figures and featured four superheroes: Batman, Superman, Aquaman, and Robin.

Not long after the launch of the first version, the second version of the World's Greatest Superheroes was launched. In addition to the aforementioned characters, the second version World's Greatest Superheroes included superheroes such as Spiderman, The Green Hornet and Captain America and villains such as the Riddler, Penguin, and Joker.

In order to market its superhero figure line to girls, Mego included female action figures to the line. The female action figures included in the line were Batgirl, Supergirl, Catwoman, and Wonder Woman. The gamble paid off and the female action figures were welcomed with open arms not just by the girls but also the boys.

In total, the World's Greatest Superheroes included thirty-three characters. In addition to the original 8" figures, bendable 5" figures and larger 12" figures were also introduced by Mego as part of its superhero figure line.

Today, the superhero figures of Mego are quite rare. So, if you have one in good condition, you may be able to earn some good money.

The Planet of the Apes and Star Trek figures of Mego

The success of World's Greatest Superheroes propelled Mego into further action and the toy manufacturing company launched two more lines of action figures, namely the Planet of the Apes figures and the Star Trek figures.

The first ever figures based on a movie series, the Planet of the Apes figures were launched by Mego in 1973. Mego's Planet of the Apes figure line included an eight-inch astronaut and four plastic primates. The success of the Planet of the Apes figure line encouraged Mego to produce more figures based on movie and TV series. This is how the Star Trek figures came about.

For Mego and fans of sci-fi shows, the Start Trek figures were pure gold. Also, just like the World's Greatest Superheroes, the Star Trek figure line included a few playsets. A version of the temple of the Vaal from "The Apple," a Transporter and an Enterprise bridge were some of the playsets included in the aforementioned line. The Star Trek figure line included many aliens and all but four of the main crewmembers. The four crewmembers not included in Mego's Star Trek line were Yeoman Rand, Nurse Chapel, Sulu, and Chekov.

Many toy companies tried to imitate the action figures of Mego but none of these figures were as successful as Mego's action figures, at least during the 70s.

The ability to recognize the value of exclusive contracts with companies was what gave Mego the edge over other toy manufacturers. By gaining exclusive rights for popular characters of the time such as the superheroes of Marvel and DC, the characters of Planet of the Apes and the protagonists and sidekicks of Star Trek, Mego put most of its competitors out of the business during the 1970s.

The Star Wars figures of Kenner

In 1977, the first ever Star -Wars film was released. After the release of the film, many cinemagoers and even some toy companies went into frenzy. Moreover, the latter found themselves in a battle to gain exclusive rights for Star Wars action figures. After gaining the rights for them, Kenner, an American toy company founded in 1947, launched the first ever Star -Wars action figures in 1978.

While most people are aware that Kenner was the first company to launch the Star Wars figures, not many know that Mego was the first company approached for the production of these figures.

Mego was made the offer before the first Star Wars film was released in 1977. Mego declined stating that it wasn't too keen to invest in every 'flash in the pan' media belonging. This was a decision that Mego lived to regret.

After Mego rejected the offer to produce the Star Wars figures, Kenner approached the relevant people for exclusive rights of the Star Wars figures. After obtaining the rights, Kenner started to produce small and cheap Star Wars action figures and it wasn't long before the toy company started to dominate the action figure market.

Seeing the success of Kenner, Mego introduced sci-fi action figures of its own such as the Black Hole figures and the Buck Rogers figures. However, none of these figures were able to unseat the Star Wars figures of Kenner from the throne.

Sought after by collectors all over the world, the Star Wars figure series launched by Kenner included characters such as "Telescoping Lightsaber" Darth Vader, Vinyl Cape Jawa, Blue Snaggletooth, Luke Skywalker, Obi-Wan Kenobi, and Han Solo.

As far as the current value of these figures is concerned, the boxed-versions of the first Star Wars figures are worth hundreds of dollars today.

The Six Million Dollar Man and Battlestar Galactica action figures

The Six Million Dollar Man action figure is probably the best representation of a one-man army figure. In fact, many people call the Six Million Dollar Man the first true action figure for boys. Many companies including Hasbro fought with Kenner to get exclusive rights for the Six Million Dollar Man action figure. However, Kenner fought off the challenge from its competitors and launched the Six Million Dollar Man action figure for the very first time in 1975.

Another action figure series that became popular during the 70s was Mattel's Battlestar Galactica. Launched in 1978, the first series of Galactica included six figures. The popular figures of this series included the Daggit action figure, the Commander Adama figure, and the Lt. Starbuck figure. The Daggit figure was launched in two variations, one with tan plastic, and the other with light brown plastic.

The aforementioned action figures were loved and adored by the kids of the 70s. Action figures resembling characters of popular films and T.V series stayed a hit among kids and even some adults all through the 70s. However, the launch of the World Wrestling Federation or WWF in 1980 changed that forever. The 80s era and the emergence of wrestling figures is what we're going to discuss next.

Figures 80s

Ah, the 80s! The 1980s was a good time to grow up. In fact, 80s kids were the lucky ones: they wore the first Nike Air Sock Racer sneakers, watched Michael Jackson perform his dance moves live, played on the first ever home consoles and saw Hulk Hogan and Rowdy Roddy piper wrestle during their prime.

In addition to the aforementioned things, 80s was a time when kids had loads and loads of action figures to play. Some of the popular action figures of the 80s included the Transformers, the Thundercats, Teenage Mutant Ninja Turtles, Silverhawks, Marvel heroes, and Micronauts. However, the action figures of the 80s that stood head and shoulders above the rest were the WWF wrestling figure.

While they existed prior to it, the 80s was when wrestling figures became popular as action figures. Most of the credit for this goes to the World Wrestling Entertainment or WWE, known as the World Wrestling Federation or WWF during its initial years.

Before we discuss which wrestling figures were adored by the kids of the 80s, let's take a brief look at the history of WWE including how it came into being and what role it's played in the popularity of wrestling.

A brief history of World Wrestling Entertainment (WWE)

Vince and Linda McMahon founded the World Wrestling Entertainment or WWE on February 21, 1980. The World Wrestling Entertainment or WWE is the name of both a privately owned entertainment company and a professional wrestling competition.

The origins of the WWE go way back to the start of the 1950s when Vincent's Grandfather Roderick McMahon created the Capitol Wrestling Corporation Limited (CWC). In 1953, CWC became part of the National Wrestling Alliance (NWA). This was the first step taken towards the establishment of the WWE.

In 1954, Roderick McMahon passed away and his son Vincent James took control of the Capitol Wrestling Corporation Limited (CWC). Vincent took CWC to new heights and not long after assuming control, he helped the company to gain 70% of the NWA's booking.

After a dispute over wrestler Buddy Rodger with NWA, Vincent McMahon ended his association with the latter in 1963. Soon after, he formed the WWWF. Compared to other pro wrestling competitions in the country, WWWF was run in a conservative manner under Vincent McMahon. Unlike other pro wrestling competitions that ran on a weekly or bi-weekly basis, the WWWF was held as a monthly event.

In 1970, the WWWF won a television program deal and in 1979, it was renamed as the World Wrestling Federation (WWF).

In the same year, Vincent J's son Vincent K McMahon and his wife Linda established Titan Sports Inc. In 1982, Vincent K McMahon bought Capitol

Wrestling Corporation Limited (CWC) from his father, seizing complete control of the company.

Vincent K McMahon wanted to make the WWF the premier wrestling competition in the country. To achieve this objective, McMahon worked tirelessly to get WWF broadcasted on major sports channels all across the United States. However, what really changed the game for McMahon was the inclusion of wrestling talents such as the Hulk Hogan and Roddy Piper in the WWF.

Soon after the inclusion of Hulk Hogan and Roddy Piper in the WWF, other wrestlers joined the pro-wrestling competition established by Vincent K. Mahon. Some of the notable names include Ricky Steamboat, Greg Valentine, Paul Orndorff, Junkyard Dog, Nikolai Volkoff, The Iron Sheik, Don Muraco, and Jimmy Snuka.

Over time, more and more wrestling talent left the AWA and NWA for WWF. It wasn't long before McMahon's dream of making the WWF the premier wrestling competition in the country came true.

The World Wrestling Federation or WWF continued to grow during the 80s, mostly due to the babyface hero Hulk Hogan. WWF secured a deal with MTV for its coverage and hosted celebrities such as Cyndi Lauper, Muhammad Ali, and Mr. T on its platform. However, the thing that aided the popularity of WWF more than anything else was the introduction of WWF wrestling figures.

Wrestling figures: how it all started

No matter how hard you try, you can't escape pro-wrestling. Once a fan, always a fan: it's that simple! Most of the wrestling fans are people who grew up in the 80s and 90s. Know the reason why? If you don't know the reason for the above then quite frankly, you've been living under a rock.

Yes, wrestling was famous before 80s but it was in the 80s that wrestling, in particular pro-wrestling, really took off. The introduction of the WWF and the advent of wrestling figures resembling the WWE stars were two major reasons for the surge in the popularity of pro-wrestling.

If you were a kid in the 80s then LJN's wrestling figures are something you'll definitely know about. During the 80s, the popularity of pro-wrestling increased significantly. This was largely due to the introduction of the World Wrestling Federation (WWF).

Seeing this surge in popularity of pro-wrestling, Titan Sports, the company owning WWF, contracted LJN to produce the first ever pro-wrestling figures in 1984. The wrestling figures produced by LJN resembled the wrestling stars of the WWE, most notably the Hulk Hogan.

Made out of solid rubber, the wrestling figures of LJN were an immediate hit with kids and even some adults. As the wrestling figures continued to increase in popularity, more and more wrestling figures were produced during the 80s. Some of those figures are considered as collector's gold today.

For 80s kids, the WWF wrestling stars were much more than just wrestlers. In fact, many of the 80s kids considered the WWF stars as their role models. It wouldn't be farfetched to say that without the LJN wrestling figures, kids of the 80s wouldn't be what they are today.

Talking about the LJN wrestling figures of the 80s, some figures were more popular than the others. These were figures that every kid wanted. So what are the figures I'm referring to? Here are six LJN figures that almost every kid in the 80s wanted. Let's roll!!

Hulk Hogan

Did you doubt that the LJN Hulk Hogan figure wouldn't make the list? If yes then I'm pretty sure you're not a 80s kid. No 80s kid in their right mind would discount the importance of LJN's Hulk Hogan figure. The Hulk Hogan figure of LJN is pure gold even today. Whether it was the series 1 figure, the 15" figure, or a bendie, LJN's Hulk Hogan figure was loved by kids of all ages during the 80s.

As for the current value of the LJN Hogan figure, the price varies based on the design, series, and size of the figure. The current value of Hulk Hogan series 1 figure with no shirt is $50. The 15" is valued at $200. The prices of the Hulk Hogan Series 5 figures are considerably high. The Series 5 Hulk Hogan figure with white shirt is valued at $335 while the Hulk Hogan figure with red shirt is available for $375. As for the Hulk Hogan Bendies figure, you can get it for $16

Andre the Giant

No 80's wrestling figure collection can be complete without Andre the Giant. Unlike the real life Andre the Giant, the figure resembling the giant was in great shape. However, the figure did have fat and bloated arms, much like the real life Andre the Giant. Though the figure I'm referring to is the Andre the Giant with short hair. There were other versions of the figure too. Some of them depicted Andre the Giant better than the short-haired Andre the Giant figure.

Today, the shorthaired Andre the Giant series 3 figure is valued at $75. The Andre the Giant figure with long hair that was produced as part of the series 1- figures is currently priced at $60. If you're a fan of the Series 6 Andre the Giant figure with black suit then you can get the figure for $240.

Adrian Adonis

Adrian Adonis wasn't part of the first three figure series released by LJN. The first and only LJN series the Adrian Adonis figure was part of was series 4. In spite of this, Adrian Adonis was a famed figure during the 80s. An 8" figure, the Adrian Adonis figure was a favorite of quite a few kids. However, there were many kids who wanted to stay far away from this 'strange looking' doll. This is one of the reasons the series 4 Adrian Adonis figure is currently valued at only $35.

Randy Savage

Whether you grew up in the 80s, the 90s or even the 2000s, you can't be a true pro-wrestling fan unless and until you know about randy savage. Only a few, if any, wrestlers commanded the same stature in their prime as 'Macho man' Randy Savage. For many years, Randy Savage was a people's favorite. The popularity of Randy Savage encouraged LJN to produce a figure resembling him. The Randy Savage wrestling figure was released as part of the LJN series 3 figures. The Randy Savage wrestling figure was part of the wrestling figure collection of most kids. Today, you can get this figure for $40.

Special Delivery Jones

Although he wasn't as famous as the wrestlers mentioned above, special delivery or S.D Jones had a significant fanbase. He was the underdog that many wrestling fans wanted to see become a top dog. Unfortunately for them, that did not happen. Nevertheless, special delivery Jones is still remembered by the kids of 80s, especially those who played with Special deliver Jones figure.

The underdog, the Special delivery Jones figure fought many fake fights and won almost all of them. The Special delivery Jones figure was released for the first time as part of the LJN series 2 figures. The first S.D Jones figure to be released was the S.D Jones figure with red figure. Today, the figure is valued at $30. The second and final Special delivery Jones figure released by LJN was the series 3 S.D Jones figure with yellow shirt. Today, you can buy this figure for $40.

Honky Tonk Man

The Elvis impersonator of the WWF, Honky Tonk Man. It wouldn't be wrong to say that Honky Tonk Man added glamour to the WWF. As far as his wrestling abilities are concerned, he wasn't much to note about. He lost most of his matches and was almost always 'outwrestled' by his opponents. Nevertheless, he was a fascinating character and this was what propelled LJN to produce his figure as part of its series 6 figures. The current value of the Honky Tonk Man figure is $225.

There you have it—six of the very best LJN 80s wrestling figures. If you currently own any of the aforementioned figures then you stand to earn a fortune. To help you find out the worth of your 80's LJN figure, following is a complete list of 80s LJN figures with their prices.

1984 LJN Series 1

Figure | Price

Andre The Giant (Long Hair): $60.00
Big John Studd: $42.00
Hillbilly Jim: $30.00
Hulk Hogan: $50.00
Iron Sheik: $30.00
Junk Yard Dog: $35.00
Jimmy "Superfly" Snuka: $65.00
Nikolai Volkoff: $35.00
Rowdy Roddy Piper: $52.00

1985 LJN - 15" Figures
Hulk Hogan: $100.00
"Rowdy" Roddy Piper: $165.00

1985 LJN Series Series 2
Brutus Beefcake: $35.00
George "The Animal" Steele: $30.00
Greg "the Hammer" Valentine: $35.00
King Kong Bundy: $40.00
Paul "Mr.Wonderful" Orndorff: $35.00
Special Delivery Jones (red shirt): $30.00

1986 LJN Series 3
Andre the Giant (Short Hair): $75.00+
Bobby "the Brain" Heenan: $40.00
Bruno Sammartino: $40.00
Captain Lou Albano: $30.00
Corporal Kirchner: $30.00
The Magnificent Muraco: $35.00
Terry Funk: $45.00
Classie Freddie Blassie: $40.00

Jessie "The Body" Ventura: $150.00
Jimmy "Mouth of the South" Hart: $35.00
Randy "Macho Man" Savage: $40.00
Ricky "The Dragon" Steamboat: $35.00
SD Special Delivery Jones Yellow Shirt: $40.00
Tito Santana: $40.00

1987 LJN Series 4
Adrian Adonis: $35.00
Billy Jack Haynes: $55.00
Bret "Hitman" Hart: $375.00
B Brian Blair: $50.00
"Cowboy Boy" Bob Orton: $35.00
Elizabeth: $65.00
Hercules Hernandez: $45.00
Jake "The Snake" Roberts: $55.00
"Jumping" Jim Brunzell: $40.00
Jim "the Anveil "Neidhart: $325.00
Kamala: $70.00
King Harley Race: $260.00
Koko B. Ware: $125.00
Mean Gene: $35.00
Mr. Fuji: $35.00
Outback Jack: $50.00
Ted Arcidi $40.00

1988 LJN Series 5
Ax of Demolition: $95.00
Bam Bam Bigelow: $90.00
Hacksaw Jim Duggan: $60.00
Hulk Hogan #2(White Shirt): $235.00
Hulk Hogan #3(Red Shirt): $275.00
Johnny Valiant: $35.00
Ken Patera: $60.00
One Man Gang: $70.00
Referee $70.00 Slick: $30.00
Ric Martel: $100.00
"The Million Dollar Man" Ted Dibiase: $60.00

Vince McMahon: $40.00

1989 LJN Series 6

Andre the Giant: $140.00
Ax of Demolition: $95.00
Bam Bam Bigelow: $90.00
Big Boss Man: $90.00
Honky Tonk Man: $225.00
Hulk Hogan #4(White Shirt): $235.00
Hulk Hogan #5(Red Shirt): $275.00
Haku: $90.00
"Ravishing" Rick Rude: $75.00
Ultimate Warrior: $450.00
Warlord: $85.00

Hasbro (LJN) Sargent Slaughter Mail Away Figure: 250.00+

Sargent Slaughter is technically not part of the WWF LJN Wrestling Superstars collection. Most collectors do consider the Sargent Slaughter figure to be part of the WWF LJN Wrestling Superstars collection.

Tag Team Boxed Sets

The Hart Foundation Bret Hart & Jim Neidhart $450.00+

British Bulldogs Davey Boy Smith & Dynamite Kid $200.00+

Iron Sheik & Nikolai Voloff: $100.00

The Killer Bee's Brian Blair & Jim Brunzell: $125.00

Hulk Hogan & Hillbilly Jim: $95.00

Greg Valentine & Brutus Beefcake: $85.00

Strike Force Tito Santana & Rick Martel: $200.00

LJN Bendies

Hulk Hogan $16.00

Roddy Piper $16.00

Paul "Mr.Wonderful" Orndorff $16.00

Brutus Beefcake $16.00

Lou Albano $16.00

Hulk Hogan $16.00

Junkyard Dog $16.00

Hillbilly Jim $16.00

Iron Sheik $16.00

Nikolai Volkoff $16.00

Ricky Steamboat $16.00

Roddy Piper $16.00

Randy "Macho Man" Savage $16.00

George "The Animal" Steele $16.00

Jessie the Body Ventura $16.00

King Kong Bundy $16.00

Korporal Kirchner $16.00

Big John Studd $16.00

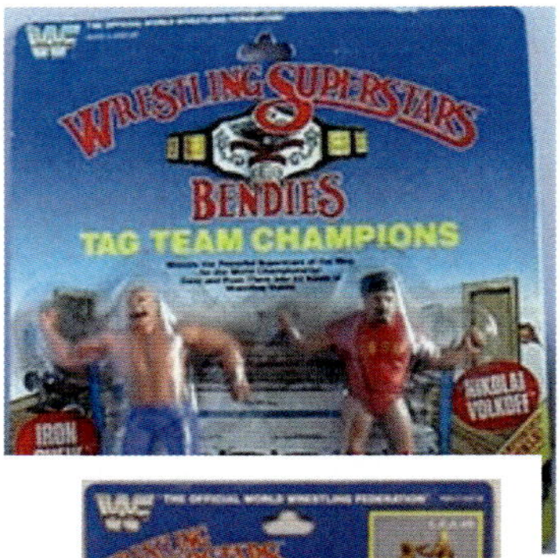

Tag Team Champions

Captain Lou and George the Animal Steele $50.00

King Kong Bundy and Big John Studd $50.00

Hulk Hogan and Junk Yard Dog $50.00

Iron Sheik and Nikolai Volkoff $50.00

Ricky Steamboat and Corporal Kirchner $50.00

Jesse Ventura and Randy Savage $50.00

WWF LJN Thumb Wrestlers (Loose Figures)

Hillbilly Jim: 15.00

Big John Studd: 15.00

Hulk Hogan: 15.00

Randy Savage: 20.00

Junk Yard Dog: 15.00

Rowdy Roddy Piper: 20.00

Iron Sheik: 15.00

Paul Orndorff: 15.00

Nikolai Volkoff: 15.00

Ricky Steamboat: 20.00
King Kong Bundy (Rare): 75.00
Jake the Snake Roberts (Rare): 100.00

WWF LJN Thumb Wrestlers (Two Packs Carded)
Jake the Snake Roberts and Ricky the Dragon Steamboat (Rare): 300.00
Paul Orndorff and King Kong Bundy (Rare): 200.00
Hillbilly Jim and Randy Savage: 100.00
Hillbilly Jim and Rowdy Roddy Piper: 100.00
Hulk Hogan and Iron Sheik: 90.00
Hulk Hogan and Big John Studd: 90.00
Hulk Hogan and Nikolai Volkoff: 90.00
Hulk Hogan and Rowdy Roddy Piper: 100.00
Hulk Hogan and Randy Savage: 100.00
Junk Yard Dog and Rowdy Roddy Piper: 100.00
Junk Yard Dog and Rowdy Roddy Piper: 100.00
Junk Yard Dog and Nikolai Volkoff: 90.00

The AWA Action figures

If you think that the WWF figures were the only wrestling figure available in the 80s then you're wrong. Another set of wrestling figures, the AWA action figures were as popular as the LJN figures during the 80s. The AWA action figures were based on wrestlers who fought in the now defunct American Wrestling Association (AWA). Made out of soft plastic, the figures had moveable heads, arms, legs, and waists.

Not many know this but the AWA action figures of Remco were the second widely produced pro-wrestling figures to hit the market. Yes, they came after the LJN' famed WWF Wrestling Superstars line. Some of the popular figures included Ric Flair, Nord the Barbarian and Greg Gagne. Following is a complete list of Remco's AWA action figures.

1985-1986 AWA Remco

Figure | Price

1985 AWA Series 1 (Tag Teams)

Fabulous Freebirds (3): $245.00
Fabulous Ones: $200.00
Gagne's Raiders: $210.00
High Flyers: $210.00
Long Riders: $200.00
Road Warriors: $220.00
Road Warriors w/ Manager: $290.00

1985 AWA Series 2 (Tag Teams)

Greg Gagne & Curt Henning: $180.00
"Wild" Bill Irwin & Scott "Hog" Irwin: $180.00
Michael Hayes, Terry Gordy & Buddy Roberts $200.00
Jimmy Garvin, Steve Regel & Precious: $200.00
Hawk, Animal & Paul Ellering: $290.00

1986 AWA Series 3 (Grudge Series)

Abdullah & Carlos Colon: $210.00
Scott Hall & Jimmy Garvin: $200.00
Nick Bockwinkle & Larry Zbyszko: $200.00
Jerry Blackwell & Stan Hansen: $210.00

1986 AWA Series 4 (Mat Mania)

Boris Zuchov: $250.00
Buddy Rose: $220.00
Doug Somers: $220.00
Nord the Barbarian: $240.00
Sheik Adnan: $250.00
Referee with Brown Hair and Referee with Grey Hair: $210.00 each
Shawn Michaels: $340.00

Marty Janetty: $220.00

1985-1986 AWA Remco Accessories
Steel cage match playset: $500.00
AWA Remco Belt: $200.00
AWA Remco Ring: $200.00

In addition to the aforementioned figures, other wrestling figures produced during the 80s included AAA by Kelian, Lucha Libre figures, and magnificent wrestler figures. We now move onto the 90s.

Figures 90s

80s saw the wrestling figures emerge and gain immense popularity. The company that benefited most from this popularity was LJN. However, in 1989, LJN shut down its toy division. Luckily, the WWF wrestling figures continued coming in. The company responsible for the production of WWF wrestling figures after the closure of LJN's toy division was Hasbro.

Hasbro produced many wrestling figures during the first half of the 1990s. However, Hasbro wasn't the only company producing wrestling figures during the 1990s. Other companies that manufactured wrestling figures in the 1990s included Jakks Pacific, ToyMakers, San Francisco Toymakers, Playmates Toy Company and Galoob. Based on their current value and popularity during the 1990s, following are the top wrestling figures of the 90s.

Hasbro's Texas Tornado

If there was any such thing as wrestling figure legends, then Hasbro's Texas Tornado would be a part of it. Part of Hasbro's series 3, the Texas Tornado figure was a figure that resembled wrestler Kerry Von Erich, better known as The Texas Tornado. Today, it is one of the rarest figures. This is the reason it's valued at $200+.

Hasbro's Kamala wrestling figure

The Kamala with the star belly was mass produced and is priced at $325 the Moon belly Kamala can reach thousands of dollars.

One of the most valuable wrestling figures of all time, Hasbro's Kamala wrestling figure came out in 1993. The figure was part of Hasbro's series 7 yellow cards line. The most noticeable feature of the figure was a moon on its belly. According to many people, the moon on the belly of Kamala was one of the reasons it became so popular. The current value of Hasbro's series 7 Kamala wrestling figure is $325.

Hasbro's Dusty Rhodes

One of the most prized wrestling collectables, the Dusty Rhodes wrestling figure of Hasbro was launched as part of Hasbro's series 2. It didn't take long for the figure to become a hit with kids. While many figures of the 90s have become rare today, the Dusty Rhodes figure was rare even in the 90s. Different people quoted different reasons for it but we won't get into the details of things.

The rarity of the Dusty Rhodes figure is the reason it's priced so high today. The present day value of Hasbro's Dusty Rhodes figure is $350+.

Hasbro's Magazine Mail-in Premiums

Hasbro's Magazine Mail-in Premiums are probably one of the most coveted wrestling collections today. The Mail-in premiums collection of Hasbro includes a Bret Hart figure with a purple heart on its gear, an Undertaker with brown hair and a Hulk Hogan with a Hulkamania shirt. Depending on their condition, the Magazine Mail-in Premiums can be worth a fortune. However, following is what the figures are currently valued at:

Mail-in Figures

Hulk Hogan: $245

Bret Hart: $250
Undertaker: $275

Hasbro's 24 Figure Collector's Case

As the name suggests, Hasbro's 24- figure collector's case was a case of 24 figures that came with their respective accessories. Part of Hasbro's series 5 figures, the 24- figure collector's case was a blue plastic case with stickers on it. The one the stickers on the case confirmed that it was an official WWF licensed product. Today, Hasbro's 24- figure collector's case is not easily available. For this reason, it's currently priced at $125.

Hasbro's Owen Hart

Manufactured by Hasbro in 1993, the Owen Hart figure was part of Hasbro's series 7 yellow cards line. The figure comes without any shirt. It was one of the rarest wrestling figures today and is valued at $175+.

Hasbro's Mr. Perfect

The Mr. Perfect figure of Hasbro was a figure that resembled the Intercontinental Heavyweight Champion Curt Hennig, better known as Mr. Perfect. The Mr. Perfect figure was part of Hasbro's series 3 -figure line. One of the most sought after figures today, the Mr. Perfect figure is currently priced at $175+.

Galoob's Big Josh

A figure that resembled WCW wrestler, Galoob's big Josh figure was part of the 1990-1991 WCW US Version figures of Galoob. If you own this figure in good condition today then you can get decent money for it. The figure is currently valued at $150.

Jakks' Razor Ramon

The final 90s figure on our list is the Razor Ramon figure of Jakks Pacific. Part of the 1996 Jakks Superstars Series 1 WWF Figures, the Razor Ramon figure is a figure that resembles a WCW wrestler of the same name. The current value of the figure is $155+

90s was a time when wrestling figures were sought after and bought by most kids. In addition to the figures of U.S based wrestlers, figures of wrestlers belonging to New Japan Pro Wrestling were also produced during the 1990s. You can find full list of 90s wrestling figures below:

Figures 2000s

Everything around us started to change after the turn of the 21st century. We had computers with high-speed internet, LCD TVs, sophisticated gaming consoles and of course, high quality wrestling figures. Talking about wrestling figures of 2000s, 2000s was when Jakks Pacific took over from Hasbro.

Jakks Pacific started its wrestling figures production in 1996 with the 'Superstars line'. The fist figures line that Jakks Pacific produced in the 2000s was the 2000 Jakks TitanTron Live Series 2 WWF "Wrestlemania". This figure line included wrestling figures such as Big Show, The Rock, and Steve Austin. This was the first of many figures series produced by Jakks Pacific during the 2000s. Apart from Jakks' Pacific figures, the wrestling figures of Mattel also became popular during the 2000s. Following are top three wrestling figures of the 2000s based on popularity and current value.

The Ultimate Warrior Limited Edition Dolls of Hasbro

In 2000, Jakks Pacific signed a contract with Ultimate Warrior to get exclusive rights for the production of his limited edition figures. The figures included 20 Unmatched Fury Warrior figures, 20 One Warrior Nation figures, 25 "Warrior America" Ring Giant figures, and 20 WCW 1998 Return figures. Additionally, Jakks Pacific produced 5 exclusive Ultimate Warrior action figures. These figures are one of the rarest figures today and can be sold by owners for as high as $1000. Below in the price guide you will find a detailed price list of the Hasbro figures with all the series listed.

Mattel's Series 1 figures

Most wrestling fans covet the series 1 figures of Mattel launched in 2010. The reason for this is the elite style and additional accessories of these figures. The series includes 6" figures of wrestlers such as Stone Cold Steve Austin, Dusty Rhodes, Sgt. Slaughter, and Road Warrior animal.

Funko Pop's Rey Mysterio Teal Pink

Manufactured in 2014, the Rey Mysterio Teal Pink is one of the most sought after wrestling figures today. The Rey Mysterio Teal Pink figure is a figure that resembles a current Mexican-American professional wrestler Óscar Gutiérrez, popularly known as Rey Mysterio. The current value of the Rey Mysterio Teal Pink figure is $100.

The aforementioned are just a few of countless figures produced in the 2000s.

Conclusion

Pro- wrestling is one of the, if not the, most popular sports in the world. The popularity of pro-wrestling is largely due to the World Wrestling Entertainment or WWE. People all around the world follow the WWE. Different people give different reasons for the success of the WWE. However, not many argue the role played by wrestling figures in WWE's success.

As mentioned earlier, wresting figures fed our obsession with pro-wrestling and made us the fans we're today. The first wrestling figures to enter our lives were LJN's wrestling figures. These are wrestling figures that we adore even today. Some of the LJN's figures loved by kids of the 80s include Hulk Hogan, Andre the Giant, Randy Savage, and special delivery Jones.

The good thing is that the Journey of Wrestling figures did not end with LJN's figures. In fact, the journey continues to date. In the 1990s, Hasbro took over from LJN and produced even better quality figures. Notable 90s figures included Texas Tornado, Dusty Rhodes, Owen Hart, and Razor Ramon.

2000s came and Mattel took over the responsibility. However, other companies have also manufactured wrestling figures from 2000 to date. Apart from helping you relive your childhood, the 80s and 90s figures mentioned in this guide can make you a fortune.

Refer to the **bonus price list supplement below** to find how much your wrestling figure is worth or how much you'll need to pay to get that coveted wrestling figure!

The Price Guide

In this book, we looked briefly at the most popular wrestling figures of the 80s, 90s and 2000s. These figures were part of many different figure series including the 1980s LJN figure series, the 1990s Jakks WWF figures series, the 2000s Jakks TitanTron series, the 1990s Kay Bee Special Edition Series, the 1990s Jakks S.T.O.M.P Series, the 1990s Hasbro series and the 2000s figures collection by Mattel.

In addition to these figures, the other wrestling figures to hit the market were the new Japan pro wrestling figures, the Lucha Libre figures, the Jesse Venture figures, the ECW figures, the WCW figures and the Bend-Ems.

Following is a complete list of wrestling figures with their prices.

Wrestling Figures

Item | Price

1996 Jakks Superstars Series 1 WWF Figures

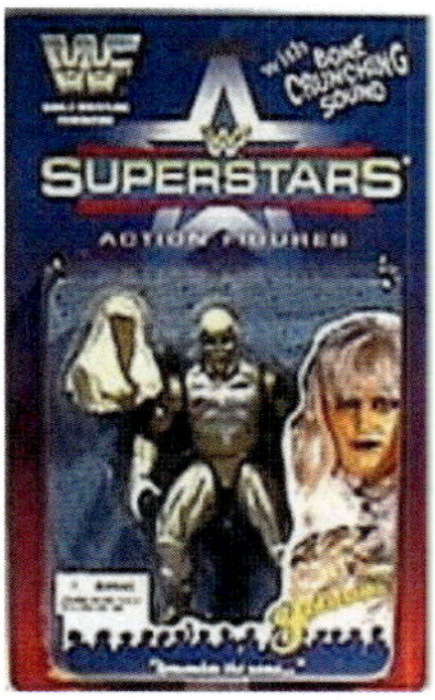

Undertaker: $15.00
Shawn Michaels: $20.00
Razor Ramon: $50.00+
Bret Hart: $25.00
Diesel: $20.00
Gold Dust: $15.00

1996 Jakks Superstars Series 2 WWF Figures

Bret "The Hit Man" Hart: $10.00
Owen Hart: $25.00+
Shawn Michaels (pink tights): $10.00
Ultimate Warrior (blue tights): $30.00
Undertaker - Glow-in-the-Dark Flesh: $25.00
Undertaker: $10.00
Vader: $10.00
4 Pack Ltd. Edition: $30.00

1997 Jakks Superstars Series 3 WWF Figures

Ahmed Johnson: $8.00
Ahmed Johnson - Rectangle Card: $8.00
Bret "The Hit Man" Hart: $6.00
Bret "The Hit Man" - Hart Rectangle Card: $8.00
British Bulldog - Rectangle Card: $8.00
Mankind: $10.00
Mankind - Rectangle Card: $8.00
Shawn Michaels: $15.00
Shawn Michaels - Rectangle Card: $8.00
Sycho Sid: $9.00
Sycho Sid - Rectangle Card: $9.00

1997 Jakks Superstars Series 4 WWF "Bad Boys" Figures
Faarooq: $6.00
Hunter Hearst-Helmsley: $6.00
Jerry "The King" Lawler: $6.00
Justin "Hawk" Bradshaw: $6.00
"Stone Cold" Steve Austin: $15.00
Vader: $8.00

1998 Jakks Superstars Series 5 WWF Figures
Flash Funk: $6.00
Sycho Sid: $6.00
Rocky Maivia: $6.00
Savio Vega: $6.00
Ken Shamrock: $6.00
Steve Austin: $6.00

1998 Jakks Superstars Series 6 WWF Figures
Black Hart Owen Hart: $50.00
Double J, Jeff Jarrett: $6.00
HHH: $6.00
Lethal Weapon Steve Blackman: $6.00
Mark Henry: $15.00
Marvelous Marc Mero: $12.00

Action Rings w/ 3" Figures
King of the Ring Action Ring with Figures: $10.00
Raw is War: $8.00
Royal Rumble: $8.00
Survivor Series: $8.00
Wrestlemania: $8.00

Best of 97 - Set 1

Bret Hart with vest: $8.00

British Bulldog with vest: $8.00

Owen Hart with vest: $8.00

Undertaker: $12.00

Best of 97 - Set 2

Crush (blue outfit): $10.00

Goldust: $9.00

Rocky Maivia: $8.00

Ken Shamrock: $18.00

1998 Jakks Superstars Series 7"Wrestle Mania XV" Figures

Dr. Death: $6.00

Edge: $10.00

"Stone Cold" Steve Austin: $10.00

Undertaker: $8.00

Val Venus: $15.00

X-Pac: $8.00

1998 Jakks Superstars Series 8 WWF "King of the Ring" Team Corporate

Big Boss Man: $8.00

Kane: $8.00

Shawn Michaels: $8.00

Ken Shamrock: $8.00

Shane McMahon: $8.00

The Rock: $8.00

1999 Jakks Superstars Series 9 WWF Figures
Paul Wight: $8.00
Bob Holly: $8.00
Christian: $8.00
Gangrel: $8.00
Undertaker: $8.00
Vince McMahon: $8.00

Best of 98 - Set 1
"Stone Cold" Steve Austin: $8.00

Best of 98 - Set 2
Dan Severn: $8.00
Dude Love: $8.00
HHH: $8.00
Ken Shamrock: $8.00
Mark Henry: $8.00
"Stone Cold" Steve Austin: $8.00
Undertaker: $8.00

1998 Jakks Bone Crushin' Buddies Series 1
Dude Love: $20.00
Shawn Michaels: $20.00
"Stone Cold" Steve Austin: $35.00
Undertaker: $20.00

1999 Jakks Bone Crushing Buddies Series 2

Steve Austin: $20.00
The Rock: $20.00
Undertaker: $20.00
L.O.D 2000 Animal: $20.00
L.O.D 2000 Hawk: $27.00+

Boxed Sets

Attitude - 4 Pack: $30.00
Badd Blood: $60.00
Buried Aliver - 4 Pack Target Exclusive: $50.00+
Champion Title Series - 4 Pack Toys 'R' Us: $25.00
D-Generation X - 4 Pack: $25.00
Go Mental - 4 Pack: $40.00
King of the Iron Rungs - 4 Pack: $30.00
Legends Past & Present: $35.00
Mick Foley's Triple Threat: $25.00
Nation of Domination - 4 Pack Toys 'R' Us: $26.00
No Holds Barred - 3 Pack: $25.00
Off the Mat - 4 Pack: $40.00
Shotgun Saturday Night - 4 Pack: $40.00
Stone Cold Set - 3 Pack: $37.00
Survivor Series - 4 Pack Toys 'R' Us Exclusive: $75.00+
Triple Threat - 3 Pack Kay-Bee Exclusive: $28.00
Undertaker (Hills 3 Pack): $25.00
Wrestlemania XIV: $30.00

Ringside Collection - Series 1
Referee: $10.00
Sable: $12.00
Sunny: $10.00
Vince McMahon: $10.00

Ringside Collection - Series 2
Honky Tonk Man: $10.00
Jim Cornette: $8.00
Jim Ross: $8.00
Sgt. Slaughter: $8.00
Vince McMahon: $10.00
WWF Referee: $10.00

Ripped & Ruthless in Your House - Series 1
Goldust: $10.00
Mankind: $10.00
Stone Cold Steve Austin: $15.00
Undertaker: $13.00

Ripped & Ruthless - Series 2
HHH: $10.00
Kane: $25.00
Sable: $15.00
Shawn Michaels: $10.00

Shotgun Saturday Nights - 1998

Henry O. Godwinn: $6.00
Phineas I. Godwinn: $6.00
Road Warrior Animal: $6.00
Road Warrior Hawk: $6.00
Rocky Maivia: $10.00+
Savio Vega: $10.00
Stone Cold Steve Austin: $15.00+
Undertaker: $10.00+

Live Wire - Series 1

Chyna: $14.00+
Ken Shamrock: $10.00+
Mankind: $10.00+
"Stone Cold" Steve Austin: $17.00+
Undertaker: $12.00+
Vader: $8.00

Live Wire - Series 2

Man Mark Henry: $8.00
Marc Mero: $10.00+
Shawn Michaels: $10.00
The Rock: $10.00
Val Venus: $10.00
X-Pac: $10.00

Managers

Bob Backlund & Sultan: $12.00
Crush & Clarence Mason: $12.00
Mankind & Paul Bearer: $12.00
Marc Mero & Sable: $15.00

DTA Tour
Blue Blazer: $75.00+
DOA Chainz: $8.00
DOA 8-ball: $8.00
Dude Love: $8.00
Faarooq: $8.00
HHH: $8.00
Kane: $8.00
Shawn Michaels: $8.00
Vader (Wal-Mart): $8.00

Fully Loaded
Al Snow: $10.00
B.A. Billy Gunn: $8.00
HHH: $8.00
Jesse James Road Dog: $8.00
Kane: $10.00+
The Rock: $10.00

Grudge Match (1998-99)
Stone Cold vs. Shawn Michaels: $22.00
HHH vs. Owen Hart: $20.00+
Luna vs. Sable: $15.00
Marc Mero vs. Blackman: $15.00
Shamrock vs. Severn: $15.00
Stone Cold vs. McMahon: $15.00
Undertaker vs. Kane: $15.00
Vader vs. Mark Henry: $15.00

3 Packs (1998)

Wrestlemania XIV (Stone Cold, Mosh, Undertaker): $28.00

Wrestlemania XIV (HHH, Thrasher, Michaels): $25.00

1999 Jakks TitanTron Live Series 1 WWF "Survivor Series"

Steve Austin: $10.00

Undertaker: $9.00

Mankind: $10.00

Road Dogg: $9.00

The Rock: $9.00

Kane: $9.00

2000 Jakks TitanTron Live Series 2 WWF "Wrestlemania"

Big Show: $9.00

The Rock: $9.00

X-Pac: $9.00

Steve Austin: $10.00

Ken Shamrock: $9.00

Undertaker: $9.00

2000 Jakks TitanTron Live Series 3 WWF "Wrestlemania"

Chris Jericho: $15.00

Chyna: $9.00

Big Boss Man: $9.00

Steve Austin: $9.00

The Rock: $9.00

Test: $15.00+

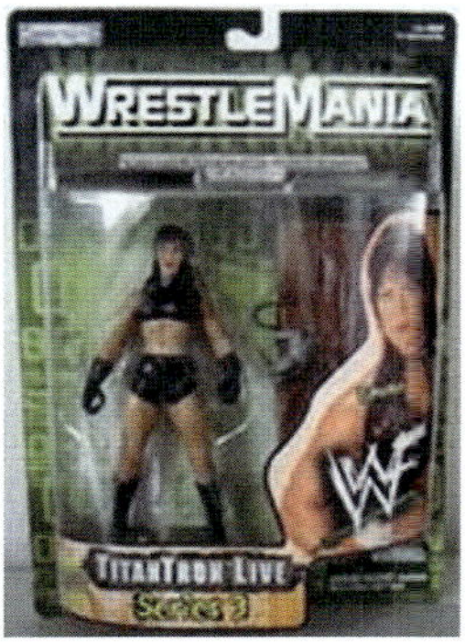

2000 Jakks TitanTron Live Series 4 WWF "Smack Down"

The Rock: $9.00

Cactus Jack: $15.00

Big Show: $9.00

Triple H: $9.00

x-Pac: $9.00

Road Dogg: $9.00

2000 Jakks TitanTron Live Series 5 WWF "Smack Down"

Kurt Angle: $9.00

Steve Austin: $9.00

Chris Jericho: $15.00

The Rock: $9.00

Undertaker: $9.00

Test: $12.00+

2000 Jakks TitanTron Live Series 6 WWF "Smack Down"

Big Show: $9.00

Triple H: $9.00

The Rock: $9.00

Edge: $10.00

Tazz: $9.00

Jeff Hardy: $9.00

2000 Jakks TitanTron Live Series 7 WWF "Smack Down"

Undertaker: $9.00

Stephanie McMahon: $9.00

Kane: $9.00

Chris Jericho: $12.00

Kurt Angle: $9.00

Triple H: $9.00

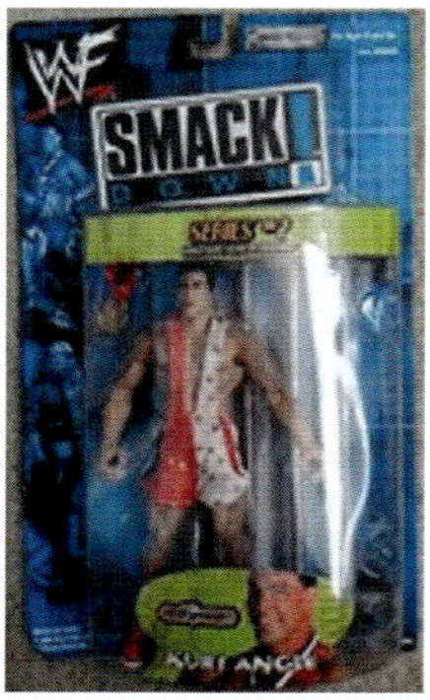

2000 Jakks TitanTron Live Series 8 WWF "Wrestle Mania"
Buh Buh Ray Dudley: $9.00
Rikishi: $9.00
Road Dogg: $9.00
The Rock: $9.00
Matt Hardy: $9.00
Jeff Hardy: $9.00

2001 Jakks TitanTron Live Series 9 WWF "Wrestle Mania"
Chyna: $9.00
Kurt Angle: $9.00
Mick Foley: $12.00
The Rock: $9.00
Rikishi: $9.00
Triple H: $9.00

2001 Jakks TitanTron Live Series 10 WWF "Heat"
Triple H: $9.00
Kane: $9.00
Rikishi: $9.00
Matt Hardy: $9.00
Billy Gunn: $9.00
Steve Austin: $10.00

2001 Jakks TitanTron Live Series 11 WWF "Heat"
Kurt Angle: $9.00
Steve Austin: $10.00
Triple H: $9.00
Jeff Hardy: $9.00
Rikishi: $9.00
Stephanie McMahon: $9.00

2001 Jakks TitanTron Live Series 12 WWF Figures

Undertaker: $9.00
The Rock: $9.00
Chris Jericho: $15.00
Big Show: $9.00
Steve Austin: $9.00
Kurt Angle: $9.00

2001 Jakks TitanTron Live Series 13 WWF Figures

Undertaker: $9.00
Triple H: $9.00
The Rock: $9.00
Lita: $9.00
Steve Austin: $9.00
Chris Jericho: $12.00
Triple H - Special Edition figure*: $15.00

Jakks Mail-Aways & Promo Exclusives

1999 White's Guide Undertaker: $25.00
1999 Toy Fare The Rock: $25.00
2000 ToyFare Debra: $20.00
2001 White's Guide Sable: $27.00
200 ToyFare Big Show: $20.00
1999 Kay Bee Steve Austin: $30.00
1999 Kay Bee The Rock: $25.00
Jakks Attitude Points Mail-Aways Kurt Angle: $20.00
Jakks Attitude Points Mail-Aways Lita: $15.00
Wizard Magazine Exclusive Steve Austin: $30.00
1999 Toy Fare Steve Austin: $25.00

1996 Jakks Series 1 Special Re-Releases
"Superstars" figure - Goldust: $25.00
Diesel: $30.00

1997 Jakks Best of Series 1 WWF "Superstars"
Steve Austin: $10.00
Ahmed Johnson: $8.00
Undertaker: $10.00
Bret Hart: $15.00
Owen Hart: $20.00
British Bulldog: $20.00

1997 Jakks Best of Series 2 WWF "Superstars"
Shawn Michaels: $10.00
Rocky Malvia: $10.00
Undertaker: $10.00
Crush: $10.00
Ken Shamrock: $10.00
Goldust: $10.00

1997 Jakks Signature Series 1
Mankind: $10.00
Animal: $10.00
Goldust: $10.00
Hawk: $20.00+
Triple H: $10.00
Steve Austin: $10.00

1998 Jakks Best of Series 1 WWF Figures

Steve Austin: $10.00
Shawn Michaels: $10.00
Chyna: $10.00
8-Bail: $10.00
Brian Christopher: $10.00
Bradshaw: $10.00

1998 Jakks Best of Series 2 WWF Figures

Steve Austin: $10.00
Dan Severn: $12.00
Jeff Jarrett: $10.00
Ken Shamrock: $12.00
Dude Love: $10.00
Undertaker: $10.00

1998 Jakks Best of Tag Teams Series 1 WWF Figures

New Age Outlaws: $20.00
Head Bangers: $20.00
Legion of Doom 2000: $25.00+

1998 Kay Bee Special Edition Series 1 WWF Figures

Sunny: $10.00
Yokozuna (red pants): $12.00
Yokozuna (white pants: $12.00
British Bulldog: $15.00
Undertaker: $10.00+
Vader: $10.00
Ahmed Johnson: $10.00
Rocky Malvia: $10.00

1998 Kay Bee Special Edition Series 2 WWF Figures

Steve Austin: $10.00
Savio Vega: $10.00
Faarooq: $10.00
Sable: $12.00
Triple H: $10.00
Goldust: $10.00

1998 Kay Bee Special Edition Series 3 WWF Figures

Hawk: $20.00
Animal: $12.00
Ken Shamrock: $10.00
Dan Severn: $10.00
Marc Mero: $10.00
Triple H: $10.00

1998 Kay Bee Special Edition Series 4 WWF Figures

Mankind: $10.00
Steve Austin: $10.00
Chyna: $10.00
Road Dogg: $10.00
Billy Gunn: $10.00
Undertaker: $10.00

1998 Kay Bee Special Edition Series 5 WWF Figures

Al Snow: $10.00
Ken Shamrock: $10.00
Edge: $12.00
X-Pac: $10.00
Val Venis: $10.00
Mark Henry: $10.00

1998 Jakks Signature Series 2
Billy Gunn: $10.00
Road Dogg: $10.00
Undertaker: $10.00
Kane: $10.00
Dude Love: $10.00
Shawn Michaels: $10.00

1999 Jakks Signature Series 3 "Wrestle Mania"
Steve Austin: $10.00
Edge: $12.00
Triple H: $10.00
Jacqueline: $10.00
The Rock: $10.00
Undertaker: $10.00

1999 Jakks Signature Series 4 - Blue Edition
Steve Austin: $10.00
Edge: $12.00
Triple H: $10.00
Jacqueline: $10.00
The Rock: $10.00
Undertaker: $10.00

1999 Jakks Sunday Night Heat
Billy Gunn: $10.00
Road Dogg: $10.00
Steve Austin: $10.00
Undertaker: $10.00
The Rock: $10.00
Sable: $10.00

1999 Jakks Signature Series 5 - Silver Edition "Survivor Series"

Al Snow: $10.00

Steve Austin: $10.00

Billy Gunn: $10.00

Big Boss Man: $12.00

Kane: $10.00

Road Dogg: $10.00

1999 Jakks Signature Series 5 - Gold Edition - Last Bone Crunching Series

Steve Austin: $10.00

Bob Holly: $10.00

Triple H: $10.00

Undertaker: $10.00

Vince McMahon: $10.00

Mankind: $10.00

1999 Jakks S.T.O.M.P Series 1

Ahmed Johnson: $10.00

Steve Austin: $10.00

Crush: $10.00

Brian Pillman: $15.00

Ken Shamrock: $10.00

Undertaker: $10.00

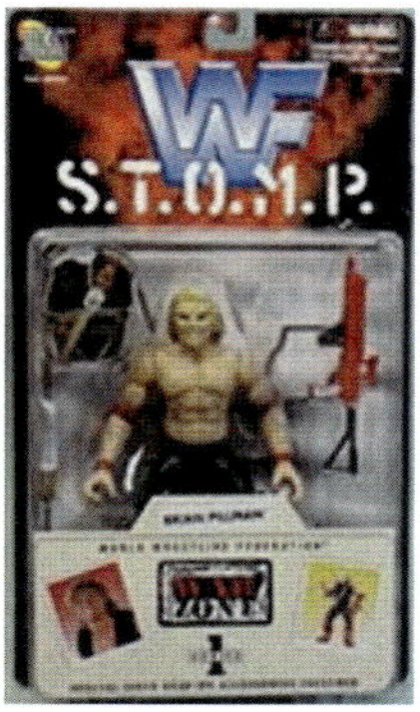

1999 Jakks S.T.O.M.P Series 2

Steve Austin: $10.00

Chyna: $10.00

Mosh: $10.00

Rocky Malvia: $10.00

Trasher: $10.00

Owen Hart: $15.00+

1999 Jakks S.T.O.M.P Series 3

Animal: $10.00
Hawk: $15.00+
Kane: $10.00
Marc Mero: $10.00
Undertaker: $10.00
Sable: $10.00

1999 Jakks S.T.O.M.P Series 4 - Camo Carnage

Steve Austin: $10.00
Chyna: $10.00
Road Dogg: $10.00
Billy Gunn: $10.00
Triple H: $10.00
X-Pac: $10.00

1999 Jakks S.T.O.M.P Series 5 - Camo Carnage (without guns)

Steve Austin: $10.00
Chyna: $10.00
Road Dogg: $10.00
Billy Gunn: $10.00
Triple H: $10.00
X-Pac: $10.00

1999 Jakks S.T.O.M.P Series 6 - Camo Carnage Special Issue

Steve Austin: $10.00
Chyna: $10.00
Road Dogg: $10.00
Billy Gunn: $10.00
Triple H: $10.00
X-Pac: $10.00

2000 Jakks Super Stunners
Christian: $12.00
Edge: $12.00
Undertaker: $10.00
Kane: $10.00
Steve Austin: $10.00
Gangrel: $10.00

2000 Jakks Back Alley Street Fighters
The Rock: $10.00
Triple H: $10.00
Steve Austin: $10.00
X-Pac: $10.00
Hardcore Holly: $10.00
Road Dogg: $10.00

1998 Jakks Slammers Series 1
Steve Austin: $10.00
Bret Hart: $15.00+
Faarooq: $10.00
Goldust: $10.00
Mankind: $10.00
Undertaker: $10.00

1998 Jakks Slammers Series 2
Dude Love: $12.00
Kane: $10.00
Shawn Michaels: $10.00
Brian Pillman: $15.00+
Taka: $10.00
The Patriot: $10.00

1998 Jakks Shotgun Saturday Night Series 1
Phineus Godwin: $10.00
Undertaker: $10.00
Henry Godwin: $10.00
Rocky Malvia: $10.00
Savio Vega: $10.00
Steve Austin: $10.00

1998 Jakks Shotgun Saturday Night Series 2
Sable: $10.00
Shawn Michaels: $10.00
Kane: $10.00
Road Dogg: $10.00
Billy Gunn: $10.00
Jeff Jarrett: $10.00

2001 SummerSlam Limited Edition
Steve Austin: $10.00
Edge: $12.00
The Rock: $10.00
Test: $12.00+
X-Pac: $10.00

1999 Jakks Wrestlemania 14
Steve Austin: $10.00
Shawn Michaels: $10.00
Triple H: $10.00
Rocky Malvia: $10.00
Mosh: $10.00
Trasher: $10.00

1999 Jakks Live Wire Series 1
Mankind: $10.00
Undertaker: $10.00
Ken Shamrock: $10.00
Chyna: $10.00
Steve Austin: $10.00
Vader: $10.00

1999 Jakks Live Wire Series 2
Mark Henry: $10.00
Marc Mero: $10.00
Val Venis: $10.00
The Rock: $10.00
Shawn Michaels: $10.00
X-Pac: $10.00

1999 Jakks Fully Loaded Series 1
Kane: $10.00
Al Snow: $10.00
Billy Gunn: $10.00
Triple H: $10.00
Road Dogg: $10.00
The Rock: $10.00

1999 Jakks Fully Loaded Series 2
Steve Austin: $10.00
Road Dogg: $10.00
The Rock: $10.00
Test: $12.00
X-pac: $10.00
Shane McMahon: $10.00

1999 Jakks Don't Trust Anybody Series 1

Faarooq: $10.00
Triple H: $10.00
Kane: $10.00
Shawn Michaels: $10.00
Dude Love: $10.00
Chainz: $10.00
Vader: $10.00
8-Ball: $10.00

1999 Jakks Don't Trust Anybody Series 2

Blue Blazer: $30.00+
Jeff Jarrett: $10.00
Steve Blackman: $10.00
Edge: $12.00
Undertaker: $10.00
Al Snow: $10.00

1999 Jakks Don't Trust Anybody Series 3

Steve Austin: $12.00
X-Pac: $10.00
Triple H: $10.00
Christian: $12.00
Ken Shamrock: $10.00
Godfather: $10.00

Jakks Ringside Series 1

Sable: $9.00
Sunny: $9.00
Vince McMahon: $10.00
Referee: $9.00

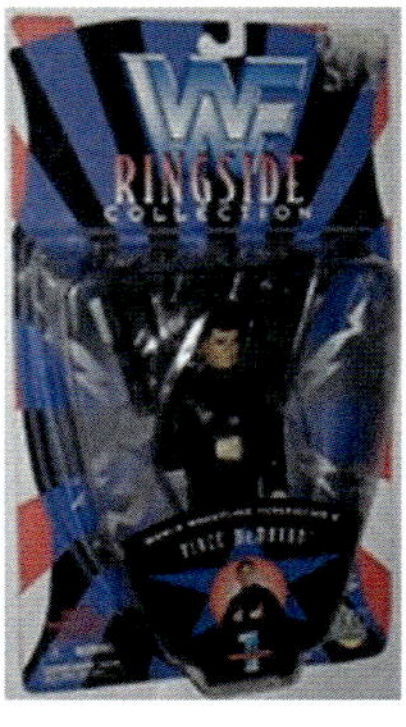

Jakks Ringside Series 2
Jim Cornette: $9.00
Sgt.Slaughter: $9.00
Honky Tonk Man: $9.00
Vince McMahon: $9.00
Referee: $9.00
Jim Ross: $10.00

1999 Jakks Break Down in Your House "King of the Ring" figures
Steve Austin: $9.00
B'Lo Brown: $9.00
Droz: $9.00
Goldust: $9.00
Mankind: $9.00
x-Pac: $9.00

1999 Jakks Raw is War
Steve Austin: $9.00
Undertaker: $9.00
Mankind: $9.00
The Rock: $9.00

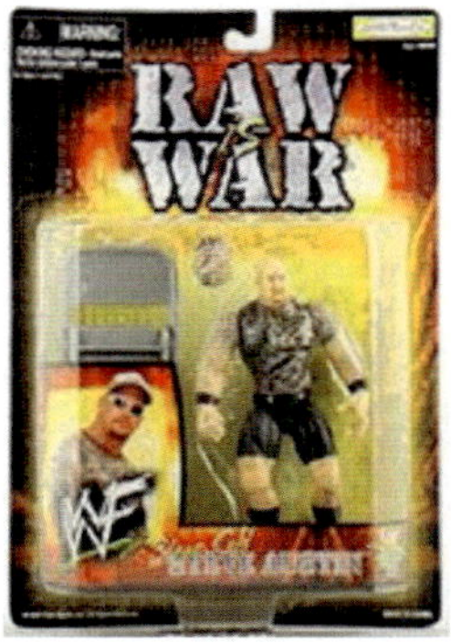

2000 Jakks Rulers of the Ring Series 1 "Wrestlemania"
Al Snow: $9.00
Edge: $12.00
Ivory: $9.00
Tazz: $10.00
Buh Buh Ray Dudley: $9.00
D-Von Dudley: $9.00

2000 Jakks Rulers of the Ring Series 2 "Smack Down"

Steve Blackman: $9.00
Big Boss Man: $9.00
Rikishi: $9.00
Scotty 2 Hotty: $9.00
Crash Holly: $9.00
Grand Master Sexay: $9.00

2000 Jakks Rulers of the Ring Series 3 "Heat"

Perry Saturn: $10.00+
Stephanie McMahon: $9.00
Eddie Guerrero: $15.00+
Prince Albert: $9.00
Raven: $12.00
Seven Richards: $9.00

2000 Jakks Rulers of the Ring Series 4

Bob Holly: $9.00
Christian: $12.00
Justin Credible: $9.00
Molly Holly: $9.00
Shane McMahon: $9.00
William Regal: $9.00

2001 Jakks Rebellion Series 1

Chris Benoit: $12.00
X-Pac: $9.00
The Rock: $9.00
Undertaker: $9.00
Jeff Hardy: $9.00
Chris Jericho: $12.00

2001 Jakks Rebellion Series 2

Kurt Angle: $9.00
Chris Jericho: $12.00
The Rock: $9.00
Crash Holly: $9.00
Undertaker: $9.00
Chris Jericho: $12.00

2001 Jakks Rebellion Series 3

Steve Austin: $9.00
Triple H: $9.00
Jeff Hardy: $9.00
D-Von Dudley: $9.00
The Rock: $9.00
Kurt Angle: $9.00

2001 Jakks Rebellion Series 4

Lita: $9.00
Billy Gunn: $9.00
Chris Benoit: $15.00+
X-Pac: $9.00
Triple H: $9.00
Edge: $12.00

2001 Jakks No Way Out Series 1

Chris Jericho: $9.00
Grand Master Sexay: $9.00
Kurt Angle: $9.00
Scotty 2 Hotty: $9.00
Steve Austin: $9.00
The Rock: $9.00

2001 Jakks No Way Out Series 2

Undertaker: $9.00
Chris Jericho: $12.00
Kurt Angle: $9.00
Matt Hardy: $9.00
Christian: $12.00
Chris Benoit: $15.00+
Lita: $9.00
Raven: $9.00
Steve Austin: $10.00

2001 Jakks Ringside Chaos Series 1

Tazz: $9.00
Steve Austin: $9.00
Scotty 2 Hotty: $9.00
Kurt Angle: $9.00
The Rock: $9.00
Undertaker: $9.00

2001 Jakks Ringside Chaos Series 2

Stephanie McMahon: $9.00
The Rock: $9.00
Steve Austin: $9.00
Chris Jericho: $9.00
Big Show: $9.00
Kurt Angle: $9.00

2001 Jakks Ringside Chaos Series 3

Steve Austin: $9.00
Eddie Guerrero: $9.00
Kurt Angle: $9.00
Steve Blackman: $9.00
Triple H: $9.00
The Rock: $9.00

1999 Jakks SmackDown TitanTron Live Series 1

Edge: $9.00
Billy Gunn: $9.00
X-Pac: $9.00
Triple H: $9.00
Gangrel: $9.00
Shane McMahon: $9.00

2000 Jakks SmackDown TitanTron Live Series 2

Steve Austin: $9.00
Road Dogg: $9.00
Edge: $12.00
Triple H: $9.00
Mankind: $9.00
Undertaker: $9.00

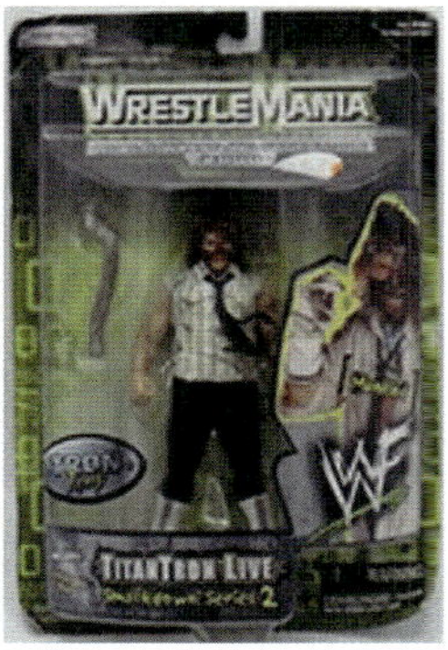

2000 Jakks Kay Bee Backlash Series 1

Steve Austin: $10.00
Triple H: $9.00
X-Pac: $9.00
Road Dogg: $9.00
Kane: $9.00
Undertaker: $9.00
The Rock: $9.00
Big Boss Man: $10.00

Shawn Michaels: $9.00
Al Snow: $9.00
Edge: $12.00+
Hardcore Holly: $9.00
Billy Gunn: $9.00

2000 Jakks Kay Bee Backlash Series 2

Hardcore Holly: $9.00
Triple H: $9.00
X-Pac: $9.00
Steve Austin: $9.00
Undertaker: $9.00
Edge: $9.00

2001 Jakks Kay Bee Backlash Series 3

Kane: $9.00
Edge: $10.00+
Billy Gunn: $9.00
Undertaker: $9.00
Triple H: $9.00
Steve Austin: $10.00
The Rock: $9.00
Big Boss Man: $9.00
Test: $11.00+_

2001 Jakks Kay Bee Backlash Series 4

Triple H: $9.00
Edge: $10.00+
Billy Gunn: $9.00
Steve Austin: $9.00
Kane: $9.00
Undertaker: $9.00
Test: $9.00
The Rock: $9.00
Big Boss Man: $10.00

2001 Jakks Kay Bee Backlash Series 5

Hardcore Holly (With Crash Holly Picture Misprint): $12.00+
The Rock: $9.00
Test: $14.00+
Undertaker: $9.00
Val Venis: $9.00
X-Pac: $9.00

2001 Jakks Signature Jams Series 1

Kurt Angle: $9.00
The Rock: $9.00
Billy Gunn: $9.00
Chris Jericho: $12.00
Triple H: $9.00
Jeff Hardy: $9.00

2001 Jakks Signature Jams Series 2

Kane: $9.00
Matt Hardy: $9.00
Undertaker: $9.00

2001 Jakks Signature Jams Series 3

Chris Jericho: $12.00
Steve Austin: $9.00
The Rock: $9.00
Undertaker: $9.00
Triple H: $9.00
Jeff Hardy: $9.00
Lita: $9.00

2001 Jakks Signature Jams Series 4
Matt Hardy: $9.00
Undertaker: $9.00
The Rock: $9.00
Steve Austin: $9.00
Jeff Hardy: $9.00
Billy Gunn: $9.00

1999 Jakks Raw Heat Series 1
Mankind: $9.00
The Rock: $9.00
Undertaker: $9.00
Steve Austin: $9.00

2000 Jakks Raw Heat Series 2 "Smack Down"
Undertaker: $9.00
Triple H: $9.00
The Rock: $9.00
Chris Jericho: $9.00
Steve Austin: $9.00

2000 Jakks Raw Heat Series 3 "Smack Down"
Matt Hardy: $9.00
The Rock: $9.00
Chris Jericho: $12.00
Steve Austin: $9.00

1998 Jakks Manager Figure Series 1

Mason & Crush: $15.00
Sable & Marc Mero: $15.00
Paul Bearer & Mankind: $15.00
Bob Backlund & Sultan: $15.00

1998 Jakks Tag Team 2 Packs

The Headbangers: $15.00
The Godwins: $15.00
Legion of Doom: $37.00+
New Blackjacks: $15.00

1998 Jakks 2 Tuff Series 1

Chyna & Triple H: $15.00
D.O.A: $15.00
Truth Commission: $15.00
Goldust & Marlena: $15.00

1998 Jakks 2 Tuff Series 2

Brian Christopher & Jerry Lawler: $15.00
Kurgann & Jackyl: $15.00
Karma & D'Lo Brown: $15.00
New Age Outlaws: $15.00

1998 Jakks 2 Tuff Series 3

Kane & Mankind: $15.00

The Rock & Owen Hart: $17.00

L.O.D 2000: $17.00+

Steve Austin & Undertaker: $15.00

1999 Jakks 2 Tuff Series 4

The Rock & Mankind: $15.00

Billy Gunn & Val Venis: $15.00

Undertaker & Kane: $17.00+

Steve Austin & Big Boss Man: $15.00

1999 Jakks 2 Tuff Series 5

Steve Austin & The Rock: $15.00

Debra McMichael & Jeff Jarette: $15.00

Viscera & Undertaker: $15.00

New Age Outlaws: $15.00

2000 Jakks Double Down Slam Series 1

Steve Austin & Shane McMahon: $15.00

Kane & X-Pac: $15.00

Shane McMahon & Undertaker: $15.00

Edge & Christian: $25.00

2000 Jakks Double Down Slam Series 2

Big Show & Steve Austin: $15.00
The Rock & Billy Gunn: $15.00
Undertaker & Kane: $20.00+
Triple H & X-Pac: $15.00

2000 Jakks Double Down Slam Series 3

Mankind & Undertaker: $15.00
Billy Gunn & Hardcore Holly: $15.00
Big Show & Test: $15.00
Steve Austin & Debra: $15.00

2000 Jakks Double Down Slam Series 4

Chyna & Chris Jericho: $15.00
Triple H & Billy Gunn: $15.00
The Hardy Boys: $50.00+

2000 Jakks Double Down Slam Series 5

Triple H & The Rock: $15.00
The Acolytes: $25.00
Edge & Christian: $50.00+

2001 Jakks Finishi Moves Series 1 WWF Figures

Olympic Slam (Kurt Angle & Chris Jericho): $15.00
Twist of Fate (Matt hardy & Jeff Hardy): $20.00
Swanton Bomb (Matt hardy & Jeff Hardy): $20.00
Pedigree (Triple H & The Rock): $15.00
Walls of Jericho (Chris Jericho & Kurt Angle): $15.00
Rock Bottom (The Rock & Triple H): $15.00

2001 Jakks Finishi Moves Series 2 WWF Figures

Choke Slam (Undertaker & Kane): $15.00
Stink Face (Rikishi & Triple H): $15.00
Tombstone (Undertaker & Kane): $15.00
Walls of Jericho (Chris Jericho & The Rock): $15.00
Pedigree (Triple H & Rikishi): $15.00
Rock Bottom (The Rock & Triple H): $15.00

2001 Jakks Finishi Moves Series 3 WWF Figures

Crossface (Chris Benoit & Chris Jericho): $20.00
Famous-er (Billy Gunn & Eddie Guerrero): $20.00
Frog Splash (Eddie Guerrero & Billy Gunn): $20.00
Twist of Fate (Matt Hardy & Jeff Hardy): $20.00
Swanton Bomb (Matt Hardy & Jeff Hardy): $20.00
Walls of Jericho (Chris Benoit & Chris Jericho): $25.00

2001 Jakks Finishi Moves Series 4 WWF Figures

Stone Cold Stunner (Steve Austin & The Rock): $15.00
Lita Canrana (Lita & Buh Buh Dudley): $15.00
Downwoard Spiral (edge & Kane): $15.00
Pile Drive (Kane & Edge): $15.00
D-Von Get the Tables (Buh Buh Dudley & Lita): $15.00
The Peoples Elbow (The Rock & Steve Austin): $15.00

1998 Jakks Thumb Wrestlers

Owen Hart & Steve Austin: $20.00

British Bulldog & Ken Shamrock: $20.00

Undertaker & Shawn Michaels: $15.00

Triple H & Mankind: $15.00

2002 Jakks Ringside Rivals Series 1

Bradshaw vs. Test: $15.00

Steve Austin vs. The Rock: $15.00

Vince McMahon vs. Shane McMahon: $20.00

2002 Jakks Ringside Rivals Series 2

Edge vs. Christian: $20.00

Kurt Angle vs. Undertaker: $15.00

Triple H vs. Steve Austin: $15.00

William Regal vs. Buh Buh Ray Dudley: $15.00

The Rock vs. Chris Jericho: $15.00

2002 Jakks Ringside Rivals Series 3

Edge vs. Christian: $20.00

Triple H vs. Kurt Angle: $15.00

D-Von Dudley vs. Spike Dudley: $15.00

2002 Jakks Ringside Rivals Series 4

Vince McMahon vs. Ric Flair: $15.00

Rob Van Dam vs. Test: $15.00

The Rock vs. Booker T: $15.00

2002 Jakks Ringside Rivals Series 5: Fatal Showdown

Undertaker vs. Hollywood Hogan: $15.00

Jeff Hardy vs. Eddie Guerrero: $15.00

Chris Jericho vs. Triple H: $15.00

2002 Jakks Ringside Rivals Series 6

Edge vs. Kurt Angle: $15.00

Test vs. Tajiri: $15.00

Rob Van Dam vs., Booker T: $15.00

2002 Jakks Fatal 4-Way Series 1

Lita: $8.00

Edge: $10.00

Jeff Hardy: $8.00

Buh Buh Ray Dudley: $8.00

2002 Jakks Fatal 4-Way Series 2

Steve Austin: $8.00
Undertaker: $8.00
Chris Jericho: $10.00
Christian: $8.00

2002 Jakks Fatal 4-Way Series 3

Chris Jericho: $10.00
Jeff Hardy: $8.00
Buh Buh Ray Dudley: $8.00
Christian: $8.00

2002 Jakks Real Reaction Series 1

The Rock: $8.00
Steve Austin: $8.00
Matt Hardy: $8.00
Chris Benoit: $10.00
Chris Jericho: $10.00
Kane: $8.00

2002 Jakks Unchained Fury Series 1 (Red Cards)

Rob Van Dam: $8.00
Booker T: $8.00
Tajiri: $8.00
Hurricane Helms: $8.00
Lance Stock: $8.00
Ric Flair: $8.00

2002 Jakks Unchained Fury Series 1 Two Packs

Booker T vs. Steve Austin: $15.00

Rob Van Dam vs. Chris Jericho: $15.00

Vince McMahon vs. Ric Flair: $15.00

2002 Jakks Unchained Fury Series 2 Two Packs

Kurt Angle vs, Edge: $15.00

Chuck Palumbo & Billy Gunn: $15.00

Diamond Dallas Page vs. Christian (1st issue): $15.00

Test vs. Christian (2nd issue): $15.00

2002 Jakks Unchained Fury Series 3

Rob Van Dam: $8.00

Booker T: $8.00

Kurt Angle: $8.00

Rhyne: $8.00

Tajiri: $8.00

Kevin Nash: $8.00

2002 Jakks nWo Series 1

Hollywood Hogan ((nWo shirt): $15.00

Hollywood Hogan (tights): $15.00

Kevin Nash (tights): $15.00

Scott Hall (nWo shirt): $15.00

Scott Hall (tights): $15.00

2002 Jakks nWo Series 1 Two Packs

Hollywood Hogan vs. The Rock: $20.00
Kane vs. Kevin nask: $20.00
Steve Austin vs. Scott Hall: $20.00

2001 Jakks Wrestlemania X-Seven Limited Edition

Steve Austin: $10.00
Edge: $12.00
Kane: $10.00
Chyna: $10.00
Eddie Guerrero: $25.00+
Chris Jericho: $25.00+

2001 Jakks Wrestlemania X-8

Rob Van Dam: $12.00
Diamond Dallas Page: $10.00
Maven: $10.00
Billy Gunn: $10.00
Chuck Palumbo: $10.00
Triple H: $10.00

2002 Jakks Superstars Uncovered Series 1

The Rock: $10.00
Hollywood Hogan: $10.00
Triple H: $10.00
Rob Van Dam: $10.00
Kurt Angle: $10.00
Undertaker: $10.00

2003 Jakks Off the Ropes
Booker T: $12.00
Edge: $12.00
Triple H: $10.00
Hollywood Hogan: $10.00
Brock Leznar: $20.00
Trish Stratus: $10.00

2002 Jakks Snapppin Bashers
Chris Jericho: $12.00
Steve Austin: $10.00
The Rock: $10.00
Jeff hardy: $10.00
Chris Benoit: $15.00
Undertaker: $10.00

2002 Jakks Royal Rumble PPV
Earl Hebner: $9.00
Tazz: $9.00
Ric Flair: $9.00
Triple H: $9.00
Willian Regal: $9.00
Chris Jericho: $9.00

2002 Jakks Match-Enders
Triple H: $9.00
Undertaker: $9.00
Edge: $9.00
Matt hardy: $9.00
Billy Gunn: $9.00
Lita: $9.00

2002 Jakks Trash Talking Champions

Chris Jericho: $9.00

Kurt Angle: $9.00

2002 Jakks Wrestling Most Wanted

Edge & Chris Jericho: $15.00

Rob Van Dam & Hardcore Holly: $9.00

Triple H & Chris Benoit: $15.00

2002 Jakks Road to Wrestlemania

Undertaker: $9.00

D-Von Dudley: $9.00

Chris Jericho: $15.00

Jeff Hardy: $9.00

Buh Buh Ray Dudley: $9.00

Chris Benoit: $15.00

2001 Jakks Final Count Series 1

The Last Ride (Undertaker & Steve Austin): $10.00

Famous-er (Billy Gunn & Matt Hardy): $10.00

Litacarana (Lita & Matt Hardy): $10.00

Downward Spiral (Edge & Billi Gunn): $10.00

Stone Cold Stunner (Steve Austin & Undertaker): $10.00

Twist of Fate (Matt Hardy & Lita): $10.00

2001 Jakks Final Count Series 2

Fist Drop (Steve Austin & Kane): $10.00

Drop Kick (Triple H & Billy Gunn): $10.00

Slam (The Rock & Chris Jericho): $10.00

2001 Jakks Final Count Series 3

Swanton Bomb (Billy Gunn & Jeff Hardy): $10.00

Clothes Line (Buh Buh Ray Dudley & Rikishi): $10.00

Walls of Jericho (Steve Austin & Chirs Jericho): $12.00

2001 Jakks Final Count Series 4

The Worm (Scotty 2 Hotty & Albert): $10.00

The Rock Bottom (The Rock & Kurt Angle): $10.00

The Unprettier (Christian & Test): $12.00

2001 Jakks Final Count Series 5

Trish Stratus vs. Jeff Hardy: $10.00

Rob Van Dam vs. eddie Guerrero: $10.00

Bradshaw vs. Undertaker: $10.00

2001 Jakks Final Count Series 6

Jungle Kick (Chuck Palumbo & Billy Gunn): $15.00

Running Leg Drop (Hollywood Hogan & Triple H): $15.00

Pedigree (Triple H & Hollywood Hogan): $15.00

Crippler Crossface (Chris Benoit & Chris Jericho): $25.00

Famous-Er (Billy Gunn & Chuck Palumbo): $15.00

Walls of Jericho (Chris Jericho & Chris Benoit: $25.00

2003 Jakks Final Count 7 Fair Punishment

619 (Rey Mysterio & Billy Kidman): $25.00

Shooting Star Press (Billy Kidman & Rey Mystero): $25.00

Tiger Bomb (Jamie Noble & The Hurricane): $25.00

Choke Slam (The Hurricane & Jamie Noble): $25.00

Sit out Power Bomb (Mark Henry & Batista): $15.00

Choke Slam (Mark Henry & Batista): $15.00

1999 Jakks Back Talking Crushers Series 1

Steve Austin: $9.00

The Rock: $9.00

Undertaker: $9.00

Big Show: $9.00

1999 Jakks Back Talking Crushers Series 2
Steve Austin: $9.00
The Rock: $9.00
Road Dogg: $9.00
Mankind: $9.00

2001 Jakks Back Talking Crushers Series 3
Triple H: $9.00
Chris Jericho: $10.00
Steve Austin: $9.00
The Rock: $9.00
Kurt Angle: $9.00

2003 Jakks Flex'Ems Series 1
The Rock: $9.00
Triple H: $9.00
Chris Jericho: $10.00
Hollywood Hogan: $9.00
Kurt Angle: $9.00
Edge: $10.00

2003 Jakks Unlimited Series 1
The Rock: $9.00
Rob Van Dam: $9.00
Chris Jericho: $10.00
Hollywood Hogan: $9.00
Kurt Angle: $9.00
Edge: $10.00

2002 Jakks Raw Draft Series

Undertaker: $9.00
Kevin nash: $9.00
X-Pac: $9.00
Scott Hall: $9.00
Kane: $9.00
Rob Van Dam: $9.00
Booker T: $9.00
Big Show: $9.00
Buh Buh Ray Dudley: $9.00
William Regal: $9.00
Lita: $9.00
Bradshaw: $9.00
Steven Richards: $9.00
Matt Hardy: $9.00
Raven: $9.00
Jeff Hardy: $9.00
Spike Dudley: $9.00

2002 Jakks SmackDown! Raw Draft Series

The Rock: $9.00
Kurt Angle: $9.00
Chris Benoit: $15.00+
Hollywood Hogan: $9.00
Billy Gunn: $9.00
Chuck Palumbo: $9.00
Edge: $12.00
Rikishi: $9.00
D-Von Dudley: $9.00
maven: $9.00
Tijiri: $9.00
Chris Jericho: $12.00+
Ivory: $9.00
Albert: $9.00
The Hurricane: $9.00
Al Snow: $9.00
Lance Storm: $12.00+
Diamond Dallas Page: $9.00

2000 Jakks House of Pain

Tori: $9.00
The Tock: $9.00
Undertaker: $9.00
Triple H: $9.00
X-Pac: $9.00
Steve Austin: $9.00

2002 Jakks Ring Leaders

The Rock: $9.00
Triple H: $9.00
Hollywood Hogan: $9.00
Undertaker: $9.00
Chris Jericho: $12.00+

2002 Jakks Rollin Rebles Vehicle

Hollywood Hogan: $25.00
Undertaker: $25.00

2002 Jakks Backlash

The Rock: $9.00
Triple H: $9.00
Kurt Angle (Bald Head): $9.00
Jeff Hardy: $9.00
Edge: $10.00
Chris Benoit: $15.00+

2002 Jakks Back Talkin' Slammers Series 3

Triple H: $9.00
The Rock: $9.00
Steve Autin: $9.00
Chris Jericho: $12.00+
Undertaker: $9.00
Kurt Angle: $9.00

2002 Jakks Back Talkin' Slammers Series 4

Triple H: $9.00
Chris Jericho: $12.00
Kurt Angle: $9.00

2003 Jakks Unrelenting

Edge: $10.00
Booker T: $10.00
Chris Jericho: $12.00
Rob Van Dam: $9.00
Jeff Hardy: $9.00
Triple H: $9.00

2003 Jakks Ruthless Aggression Series 1

Rey Mysterio: $10.00
Brock Lesnar: $20.00+
Chavo Guerrero: $12.00
Eric Bischoff: $9.00
John Cena: $9.00
Randy Orton: $10.00

2000 Jakks SmackDown! Microphone & Belt Edition

Steve Austin: $9.00
The Rock: $9.00
Undertaker: $9.00
Big Show: $9.00

1998 Jakks Bone Crunching Buddies Series 1

Shawn Michaels: $9.00
Steve Austin: $9.00
Dude Love: $9.00
Undertaker: $9.00

1998 Jakks Bone Crunching Buddies Series 2

Steve Austin: $9.00
The Rock: $9.00
Undertaker: $9.00
L.O.D 2000 Hawk: $15.00+
L.O.D 2000 Animal: $9.00

1998 Jakks Legend Series

Andre the Giant: $15.00
Jimmy Snuka: $15.00
Lou Albano: $15.00
Freddit Blassie: $15.00

1998 Jakks Ripped & Ruthless Series 1
Steve Austin: $9.00
Mankind: $9.00
Undertaker: $9.00
Goldust: $9.00

1998 Jakks Ripped & Ruthless Series 2
Triple H: $9.00
Sable: $9.00
Shawn Michaels: $9.00
Kane: $9.00

1998 Jakks Ripped & Ruthless Fantasy Warfare Exclusives
Steve Austin vs. Andre the Giant (Target): $9.00

2001 Jakks Federation Fighters 12 inch Dolls Series 1
The Rock: $9.00
Undertaker: $9.00
Steve Austin: $9.00
Kane: $9.00
Steve Austin (Camo): $9.00

2001 Jakks Federation Fighters 12 inch Dolls Series 2

The Rock: $10.00

Undertaker: $10.00

Steve Austin: $10.00

Big Show: $10.00

2001 Jakks Ringside Rebels 12 inch Dolls Series 1

The Rock: $10.00

Undertaker: $10.00

Steve Austin: $10.00

2001 Jakks Ringside Rebels 12 inch Dolls Series 2

The Rock: $10.00

Chris Jericho: $15.00

Triple H: $10.00

2001 Jakks Ringside Rebels 12 inch Dolls Series 3

Booker T: $10.00

Rob Van Dam: $10.00

Triple H: $10.00

2001 Jakks Ringside Rebels 12 inch Dolls Series 4

Hollywood Hogan: $10.00

The Rock: $10.00

Jeff Hardy: $10.00

Jakks Grudge Match Two Packs

Dan Severn & Ken Shamrock: $15.00

Undertaker & Kane: $15.00

Triple H & Owen Hart: $20.00

Steve Austin & The Rock: $15.00

Undertaker & Paul Bearer (Bradlees Exclusive): $20.00

Razor Ramon & Diesel: $20.00

Steve Austin & Vince McMahon: $15.00

Taka & Brian Christopher: $15.00

Luna & Sable: $15.00

Vader & Mark Henry: $10.00

Shawn Michaels & Steve Austin: $15.00

Marc Mero & Steve Blackburn: $15.00

Sycho Sid & British Bulldog: $25.00

Shawn Michaels & Vader: $15.00

Mankind & Al Snow: $15.00

Big Show & Mankind: $15.00

Hardcore Holly & Al Snow: $10.00

Shawn Michaels & Triple H: $15.00

Billy Gunn & Ken Shamrock: $15.00

Billy Gunn & Road Dogg: $15.00

Triple H & The Rock: $15.00

Steve Austin & Big Show: $15.00

Road Dogg & Al Snow: $10.00

Jeff Jarrett & X-Pac: $10.00

1999 Jakks SmackDown! Two Packs

Kane & X-Pac: $10.00

Steve Austin & Triple H: $10.00

Mankind & The Rock

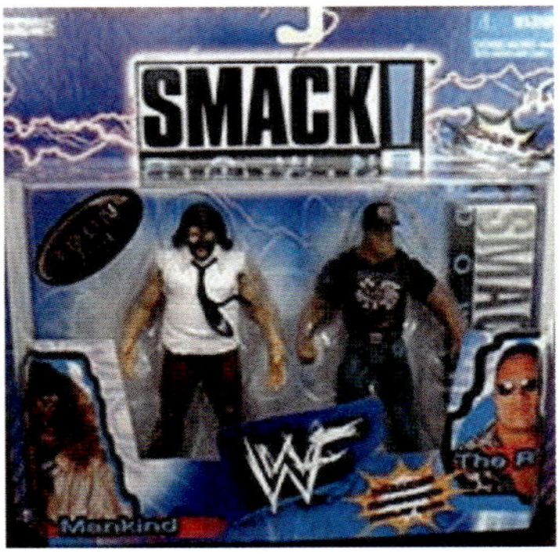

1997-1998 Jakks Best of Tag Teams

97 New Blackjacks: $15.00

97 Legion of Doom: $25.00

97 The Godwins: $15.00

97 The Headbangers: $15.00

98 The Headbangers: $15.00

98 New Age Outlaws: $15.00

1999 Jakks Wrestlemania XV Two Packs

D'Lo Brown & Mark Henry: $15.00

The Headbangers: $15.00

Mankind & Al Snow: $15.00

Jakks Boxed Sets

Brothers of Destruction (3 figures): $40.00

Renegades (3 figures): $25.00

Leap of Faith (3 figures): $50.00

Kay Bee Triple Threat (3 figures): $35.00

Billion Dollar Trio (3 figures): $25.00

DX Wise Guyz (4 figures): $40.00

Pictures perfect (2 figures): $25.00

Immortal Champions (3 figures): $25.00

Corporate Corruption (3 figures): $25.00

A Cold Day in Dudleyville (3 figures): $30.00

Get in the Groove (3 figures): $25.00

Get in the groove Variant (3 figures): $25.00

Back in the Ring (3 figures with new style Undertaker): $25.00

In the Ring Variant (3 figures with old style Undertaker): $25.00

Back in the ring 2 (3 Figures): $25.00

SmackDown! Draft (4 figures): $35.00

Raw Draft (4 figures): $35.00

Survivor Series (4 Figures): $25.00

Insurrection (U.K exclusive 10 pack): $225.00

TLC high Flyers (3 flyers): $25.00

Triple Threat (3 figures): $25.00

Attitude (4 figures): $25.00

Perfect 10 (10 pack): $150.00

Camo Carnage (3 figures): $25.00

Stone Cold Steve Austin (3 figures): $25.00

World Championship Collection (3 figures): $35.00

Wrestlemania X8 (6 figures): $75.00

No Chance (3 figures): $25.00

Fully loaded (4 figures): $25.00

Over the Edge (4 figures): $25.00

Bad to the Bonz (3 figures): $25.00

Hulk Still Rules (3 figures): $25.00

nW0 Federation Poison (3 figures): $50.00+

Razor's Edge (3 figures): $40.00+

Brass Revenge (3 figures): $25.00

Seek and Destroy (3 figures): $25.00

D-Generation X (4 figures): $50.00

Legends of the Pst & Present (3 figures): $25.00
Badd Blood (4 figures): $25.00
Triple Threat (3 figures): $25.00
Mick Foley's Triple Treat (3 figures): $35.00+
Buried Alive (4 figures): $25.00
Nation of Domination (4 figures): $25.00
Kings of the Iron Rungs (4 figures): $25.00
Survivor Series (3 Figures): $25.00
Team Xtreme (3 figures): $25.00
Shotgun Saturday Night (4 figures): $25.00
Raw is War (4 figures): $25.00
Ultimate Collection (4 pack mail-away): $80.00+
Go Mental (4 figures): $25.00
Survivor Series (3 Figures): $25.00
Wrestlemania (4 figures): $35.00
Hardcore Match (3 figures): $25.00
Last Man Standing (4 figures): $25.00
Slammers (4 figures): $25.00
Raw is War (4 figures): $25.00
TitanTron Live SmackDown! (3 figures): $25.00
Championship Title (4 figures): $30.00
No Holds Barred (3 figures): $25.00
Judgment Day (3 figures): $25.00
Off the Mat (3 figures): $25.00

Jakks BJ's Wholesale Club 3 Packs

Triple H, Mosh & Shawn Michaels (BJ's Exclusives): $25.00

Steve Austin, Trasher & Undertaker (BJ's Exclusive): $25.00

Undertaker, Val Venis & X-Pac (BJ's Exclusive): $25.00

Steve Austin, Dr.Death & Edge (BJ's Exclusive): $35.00

Triple H, Edge & Road Dogg (BJ's Exclusive): $25.00

Steve Austin, D'Lo Brown &

Droz (BJ's Exclusive): $25.00
Mankind, X-Pac & Goldust (BJ's Exclusive): $25.00

Jakks Grapple Gear Series 1
Casket Match: $10.00
Alley Match: $10.00
Commentator Booth: $10.00

Jakks Grapple Gear Series 2 (Summerslam 98)
No Pain No Gain: $10.00
Breakdown: $10.00
Hardcore Rules: $10.00

Jakks Grapple Gear Series 3 (Wrestlemania 2000)
Street Fight Rules: $10.00
Raw Live: $10.00
Backstage Brawl: $10.00
Boiler Room mayhem: $10.00
Construction Chaos: $10.00
Treacherous Training: $10.00

Jakks Grapple Gear Series 4
Top Dogg: $10.00
Parking Lot Pandemonium: $10.00
Crash n' Burn: $10.00
Game Over: $10.00
Breakdown in Your House #2: $10.00
Hardcore Recovery: $10.00

1999 Jakks Raw Heat Grapple Gear
Locker Room Rumble: $10.00
Side-Street Demolition: $10.00
Commentator: $10.00
Buried Alive: $10.00
No "DQ": $10.00
War Zone: $10.00

2001 Jakks Ring Gear Series 1
Raw Ring Skirt: $10.00
Ring Posts: $10.00
SmackDown! Ring Skirt: $10.00
Barbed Wire Bat, Cart, Belt & Tray: $10.00
Tables, Ladders & Chairs: $10.00
Scale, Belt, Cart & Fire Extinguisher: $10.00

2001 Jakks Ring Gear Series 2
Sunday Night Heat Ring Skirt: $10.00
Sunday Night Heat Ring Posts: $10.00
Door, Belt & fire Extinguisher: $10.00
File Cabinet, Belt & Table: $10.00
Ladder, Chair & Trash can: $10.00
Championship Belt: $10.00

2001 Jakks Ring Gear Series 3
Wrestlemania Ring Skirt: $10.00
Hardcore Matchup: $10.00
Hardyz Ladder Match: $10.00
Linda McMahon's Revenge: $10.00
Texas Rattlesnake: $10.00
D-Von Get the Tables: $10.00

2001 Jakks Ring Gear Series 4
Summer Slam Ring Skirt: $10.00
Tire, Pipe, Lamp & Wrench: $10.00
SmackDown! Ring Skirt: $10.00
Stretcher & Crutches: $10.00
Table, Bell & Headphones: $10.00
Video Camara & Crate: $10.00

2001 Jakks Ring Gear Series 5
Green Room: Window: $10.00
Green Room: Plant & Lamp: $10.00
Green Room: Sofa & Belt: $10.00
Table Match: $10.00
Ring Skirt: $10.00
Ladder Match: $10.00

2001 Jakks Ring Gear Series 6
Wrestlemania X8: Ring Skirt: $10.00
Wrestlemania X8: Ring Posts: $10.00
Locker Room Brawl: $10.00
Championship Title Pack: $10.00

2002 Jakks Grapple Gear Match Bits

APA Table Set: $10.00
APA Cabinet Set: $10.00
Parking Lot Set: $10.00
Backstage Security Area: $10.00
Belt Match: $10.00

2002 Jakks Septic Sludge: Gear Gone Badd Series 1

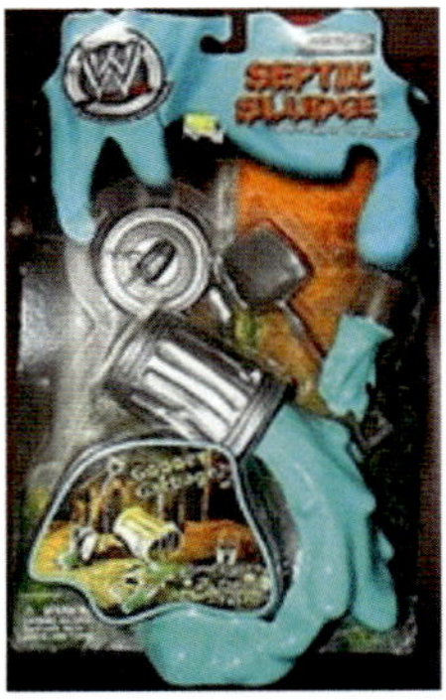

Goooey Garbage: $10.00
Lazy Janitor: $10.00
Messy Bathroom: $10.00
Oil Spill: $10.00

2002 Jakks Septic Sludge: Gear Gone Badd Series 2

Clean-Up Crew: $10.00
Concrete Jungle: $10.00
Medical Mess: $10.00
Mud Match: $10.00

Jakks Wrestling Rings & Accessories

Real Sounds Arena: $30.00
Metal Vengeance Arena: $25.00
Wrestling Ring (with twin catapults): $10.00
Backstage Mayhem: $10.00
Prop Box: $10.00
Trash Talking Stage: $10.00
Monster Ring 1996: $10.00
War Zone Monster Size Ring: $10.00

Hardcore Action Ring: $10.00
Demolition Dock: $10.00
Action Ring: $10.00
Hall of Pain: $10.00
Raw is War: $10.00
TitanTron Live: $10.00
Hardcore Action Ring (K-Mart): $10.00
SmackDown! Stage: $10.00
Stage of Rage: $10.00
Rage in the Cage: $10.00
Entrance Stage: $10.00
Backlash Action Ring: $10.00
Hall of Pain: $10.00
The New Raw Stage!: $10.00
NW0 Metal Match: $10.00
Amplified Mic: $10.00
Vince McMahon Microphone: $10.00
Backstreet Alley Playset: $10.00
Break room Brawl: $10.00

Jakks Mini Wrestling Ring Sets
Sudden Threat 1999: $25.00
Ring of Doom 1999: $25.00
Steel City 1999: $35.00
Lethal Ladder Match 2000: $25.00
No Mercy 1999: $25.00
Deadly Dungeon 2000: $25.00
Raw is War 1997: $35.00
Royal Rumble1998: $35.00
King of the Ring 1998: $35.00
Wrestlemania 1997: $35.00
Survivor Series 1998: $25.00
Buried Alive 2000: $25.00
Inferno Match 2000: $25.00

2000 Jakks Real Scan Four Pack

Kane, Steve Austin, Billy Gunn & Chris Jericho: $40.00

2002 Jakks 3 inch Slammers

Steve Austin: $8.00

The Rock: $8.00

Chris Jericho: $10.00+

Slammers Action Ring: $12.00

1999 Jakks K-Mart Grapple Gear Boxed Sets

Stone Cold Steve Austin: $8.00

The Rock: $8.00

Mankind: $8.00

Kane: $8.00

1999 Jakks Hardcore Collection Boxed Sets

The Rock (with shirt, video & mini figures): $20.00

Stone Cold Steve Austin (with shirt, video & mini figures): $25.00

ks The Rock Scorpion King & The Mummy Returns Figures

The Scorpion King: $25.00

Mathayus: $25.00

Cassandra: $20.00

Balthazar: $20.00

Jakks Rock Solid Two Packs

The Rock Figure & Scorpion King figure (real scan): $50.00

Rock Figure & The Scopion King figure (sculpted): $52.00

6.5 Inch Action Figure Belts

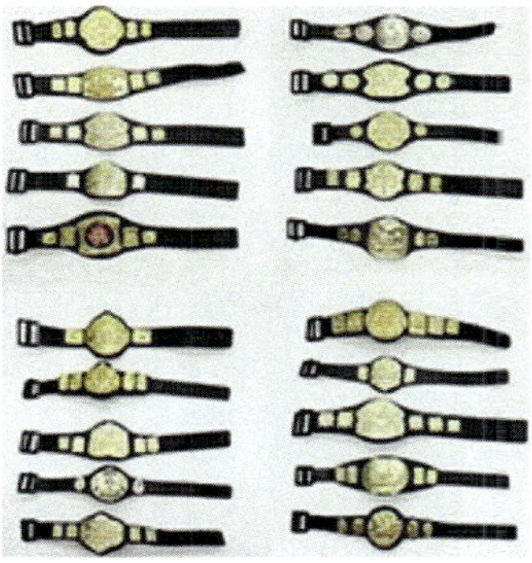

Bone Crunching World Heavyweight Title: $5.00

Bone Crunching Tag Team Title: $5.00

Bone Crunching Hardcore Title: $5.00

Hardcore Title: $5.00

TitanTron World Heavyweight Title: $5.00

TitanTron Tag Team Title: $5.00

TitanTron Hardcore Title: $5.00

TitanTron Intercontinental Title: $5.00

TitanTron Steve Austin Smoking Skull Title: $5.00

TitanTron World Heavyweight Title #2: $5.00

Figures Toy Company (1998-Present)

Item | Value

Figures Toy Company Legends of Professional Wrestling

King Kong Bundy: $14.00
King Kong Bundy (bloody version): $14.00
Abdullah The Butcher: $18.00
Abdullah The Butcher (bloody version): $18.00
Killer Kowalski: $15.00
Killer Kowalski (bloody version): $17.00
Tony Atlas: $17.00
Tony Atlas (bloody version): $15.00
Iron Sheik: $15.00
Iron Sheik (bloody version): $15.00
Old Bruno Sammartino: $18.00
Old Bruno Sammartino (bloody version): $18.00
Nikolai Volkoff: $15.00
Nikolai Volkoff (bloody version): $15.00
Greg Valentine: $15.00
Greg Valentine (bloody version): $15.00
Kamala: $15.00
Kamala (bloody version): $15.00
The Santana: $15.00
the Santana (bloody version): $15.00
Bob Orton Jr.: $15.00
Bob Orton Jr. (bloody version): $15.00
Young Bruno Sammartino: $15.00
Young Bruno Sammartino (bloody): $15.00
Lou Albano: $15.00
Lou Albano (bloody): $15.00
Ox Baker: $15.00
Ox Baker (bloody): $15.00
Billy Graham: $14.00
Billy Graham (bloody): $14.00
Chieff Jay Strongbow: $15.00
Chieff Jay Strongbow (variant version): $15.00
Ivan Koloff: $9.00

Ivan Koloff (bloody): $9.00
Baron Van Raschke: $9.00
Baron Van Raschke (bloody): $9.00
Wahoo McDaniel: $15.00
Wahoo McDaniel (bloody): $15.00
Ricky Steamboat: $20.00
Ricky Steamboat (bloody): $20.00
Eddie Gilbert: $10.00
Eddie Gilbert (bloody): $10.00
Original Sheik: $12.00
Original Sheik (bloody): $12.00
Jimmy Valiant: $10.00
Jimmy Valiant (bloody): $10.00

Figures Toy Company Legends of Professional Wrestling Multi Figure Packs

Tony Atlas vs. Billy Graham (bloody): $20.00

Abdullah The Butcher vs. Kamala (bloody): $21.00
King Kong Bundy vs. Tony Atlas (bloody): $15.00
Tito Santana vs. Greg Valentine: $15.00
Young Bruno vs. Killer Kowalski: $15.00
Abdullah The Butcher vs. Original Sheik (bloody): $15.00
Ricky Streamboat vs. Bob Orton Jr.: $20.00
Eddie Gilbert vs. Original Sheik: $15.00
Young Sammartino vs. Old

Sammartino: $15.00

Old Bruno Sammartino vs. Ivan Koloff: $15.00

Figures Toy Company Legends of Professional Wrestling Tag Team Two Packs

Ivan Putski & Tito Santana: $15.00

Ivan Koloff & Nikolai Volkoff: $15.00

King Kong kBundy & Bob Orton Jr.: $15.00

Chief Jay Strongbow & Wahoo McDaniel: $15.00

Ox Baker & Baron Von Raschke: $15.00

Ivan Koloff & Nikolai Volkoff: $15.00

Glow in the Dark Figures

Abdullah The Butcher: $15.00

King Kong Bundy: $12.00

Ivan Putski: $18.00

Killer Kowalski: $15.00

Internet Exclusives

Abdullah The Butcher: $24.00

Ivan Putski: $25.00+

Wrestling Superstore figures
Referee: $9.00
Referee (bloody): $9.00
Security Guard: $12.00
Event Staff Guard: $10.00

Hasbro Figures Guide

Item | Value

1990 Hasbro Series 1

Akeem: $45.00
Andre The Giant: $125.00+
Ax: $35.00
Big Bossman: $30.00
Brutus Beefcake: $20.00
Hulk Hogan "Gorilla Press": $27.00
Jake the Snake Roberts: $50.00
Macho Man Randy Savage: $35.00
Ted Dibiase: $30.00
Ravishing Rick Rude: $35.00
Smash: $25.00
Ultimate Warrior #1: $200.00+

1990 Hasbro Series 2

Dusty Rhodes: $350.00+
Hacksaw Jim Duggan (with 2x4): $25.00
Honky Tonk Man: $47.00
Hulk Hogan "Hulkster Hug": $30.00
Macho Man Randy Savage: $35.00
Ted Dibiase (green suit): $25.00
Rowdy Roddy Piper: $30.00
Jimmy Snuka: $20.00
Ultimate Warrior #2: $200.00+

1991 Hasbro Series 3

Big Boss Man: $20.00
Brutus Beefcake: $35.00
Earthquake: $30.00
Greg Valentine: $25.00
Hulk Hogan (Hulkaplex): $28.00
Koko B. Ware: $60.00
Mr. Perfect: $175.00
Sgt.Slaughter: $40.00
Texas Tornado: $200.00+

Typhoon: $30.00
Ultimate Warrior #3: $65.00

1992 Hasbro Series 4

British Bulldog: $50.00+
Ricky Steamboat: $40.00
Bret Hart: $55.00+
Undertaker: $30.00

1993 Hasbro Series 5

Hulk Hogan #4: $30.00
Irwin R.Shyster: $15.00
Ric "The Model" Martel: $30.00
Skinner: $15.00
Sid Justice: $30.00
The Mountie: $15.00
Virgil: $17.00
Warlord: $42.00
Hasbro 24 Figure Collector's Case: $125.00

1993 Hasbro Series 6

Bezerker: $16.00
Tito Santana"El Matador": $25.00
Jim Neidhart: $40.00
Papa Shango: $15.00
Repo man: $15.00
Ric Flair: $40.00
Tatanka: $15.00

1993 Hasbro Series 7 (yellow cards)
Crush: $22.00
Kamala: $225.00+
Nailz: $14.00
Owen Hart: $175.00+
Razor Ramon: $30.00
Shawn Michaels: $30.00

1994 Hasbro Series 8 (red cards)
Bam Bam Bigelow: $40.00
Bret Hart: $42.00+
Lex Luger: $35.00
Mr. Perfect: $30.00
Undertaker: $40.00
Yokozuna: $35.00

1994 Hasbro Series 9 (purple cards)
Doink The Clown: $40.00
Jim Duggan: $17.00
Ted Dibiase: $17.00
Rick Steiner: $16.00
Scott Steiner: $17.00+
Tatanka: $15.00

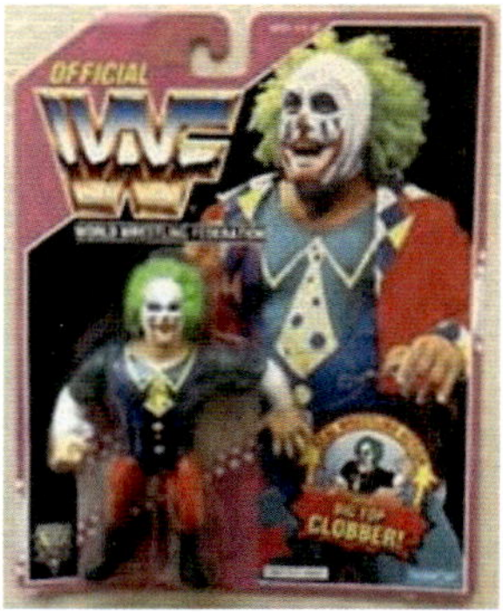

1994 Hasbro Series 10 (blue cards)
Bushwaker Butch: $16.00
Bushwaker Luke: $16.00
Headshrinker Fatu: $14.00
Headshrinker Samu: $14.00
Giant Gonzalez: $20.00
Marty Janetty: $15.00
Razor Ramon: $30.00
Shawn Michaels (red & white): $37.00

Shawn Michaels (silver & black): $25.00

1994 Hasbro Series 11 (green cards)

Yokozuna: $30.00
1-2-3 Kid: $75.00
Adam Bomb: $30.00
Smokin' Gunn Billy: $30.00
Smokin' Gunn Bart: $30.00
Crush: $30.00
Ludvig Borga: $30.00

1991 Hasbro Tag Teams

Bushwhackers: $40.00
Demolition: $65.00
Nasty Boys: $80.00
Legion of Doom: $65.00+
Rockers: $35.00

Magazine Mail-in Premiums 1992

Hulk Hogan (Hulk mania shirt): $245.00
Bret hart (Purple Heart): $350.00+
Undertaker (brown hair): $275.00

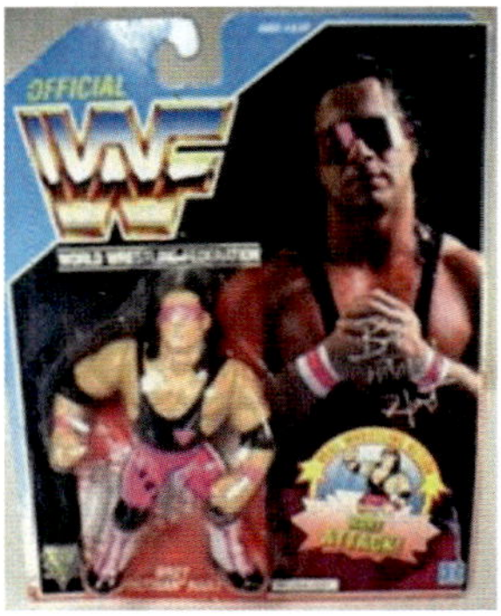

HASBRO Mail In Figures

Bret Hart - '92 Mail-In: $240.00
Hulk Hogan '93 Mail-In loose figure: $235.00
Undertaker - '93 Mail-In: $265.00
Bushwackers - 2 pack: $40.00
Demolition - 2 pack: $65.00
Legion of Doom - 2 pack: $55.00
Nasty Boys - 2 pack: $80.00
Rockers - 2 pack: $35.00

Mini-Wrestlers

Card #7391: $15.00
Card #7392: $15.00
Card #7393: $15.00

UK Exclusives

Arn Anderson (red trunks): $35.00
Barry Windham (blue trunks): $35.00
Big Josh: $90.00
Brian Pillman: $55.00
Butch Reed: $35.00
Dusty Rhodes: $90.00
El Gigante: $70.00
Jim Garvin: $70.00
Lex Luger (green trunks): $35.00
Michael Hayes: $70.00
Ric Flair (maroon trunks): $35.00
Rick Steiner (green pattern): $35.00
Ron Simmons: $35.00
Scott Steiner (pink/black): $35.00
Sid Vicious: $35.00
Sting (salmon tights): $55.00
Tom Zenk: $35.00

Freebird Set: $150.00

Original San Francisco Toy Makers

ECW 1999 Series 1
Chris Candido $25.00
Justin Credible $25.00
Rob Van Dam $25.00
Sabu $25.00
Shane Douglas $25.00

Series 2
Buh Buh Ray Dudley $25.00
D-Von Dundley $25.00
Lance Storm $37.00
New Jack $25.00
Tommy Dreamer $25.00

Series 3
Justin Credible $25.00
New Jack $25.00
Taz $25.00

Series 4 Released in Year 2000

Axl Rotten $25.00
Balls Mahoney $25.00
Jerry Lyn Raven $25.00
Rhino $25.00
Rob Van Dam $25.00
Taz $25.00
Yoshihiro Tajiri $25.00

Series 5-Bash of the Brawlers

Justin Credible $25.00
Little Guido $25.00
Mike Awesome $25.00
Nova $25.00
Sabu $25.00
Sandman $25.00
Steve Corino $25.00
Super Crazy $25.00

Series 6-Thrill Zone

Balls Mahoney $25.00
Chris Candido $25.00
Lane Storm $37.00
New Jack $25.00
Raven $25.00
Rhino $25.00
Rob Van Dam $25.00
Tommy Dreamer $25.00

WCW 1998 12 Inch Figures

Goldberg $35.00
Hollywood Hogan Figures $40.00
Macho Man Randy Savage $40.00
Sting (Black and White) $40.00
Sting (Red and Back) $40.00

WCW 1998 Series

Bret Hart (Atomic Elbow) $20.00
Chris Benoit (Double Axe Handle) $20.00
Diamond Dallas Page (Double Axe Handle) $15.00
Goldberg (Atomic Elbow) $15.00
Raven (Power Punch) $15.00
Rey Mysterio (Super Kick) $20.00
Rick Flair (Forearm Smash) $15.00
Sting (Power Punch) $15.00

WCW NWO Series 1998

Curt Henning (Atomic Elbow) $15.00
Giant (Double Axe Handle) $15.00
Hollywood Hogan (Clothes Line) $20.00
Keven Nash (Power Punch) $15.00
Lex Luger (Clothes Line) $15.00
Macho Man Randy Savage (Forearm Smash) $15.00
Marcus Bagwell (Atomic Elbow) $10.00
Scott Hall (Atomic Elbow) $15.00
Scott Steiner (Double Axe Handle) $20.00
Sting (Power Punch) $15.00

WCW 4.5 Inch Figures 1998

Goldberg $10.00
Rick Flair $15.00
Rick Steiner $15.00
Sting $15.00

WCW 4.5 Inch Figures 1998 (Two Packs)

Rick Flair and Lex Luger $25.00

Sting and Rick Steiner $25.00

WCW 4.5 Inch Figures 1998 (Four Pack)

Sting, Rick Steiner, Rick Flair, Lex Luger $40.00

WCW NWO 4.5 Inch Figures 1998

Giant $15.00

Hollywood Hogan $15.00

Kevin Nash $15.00

Lex Luger $15.00

Macho Man $15.00

Scott Hall $15.00

Scott Steiner $15.00

WCW NWO 4.5 Inch Figures 1998 (2 Packs)

Hollywood Hogan and Scott Steiner $25.00

Kevin Nash and Macho Man Randy Savage $25.00

WCW NWO 4.5 Inch Figures 1998 (Four Pack)

Hollywood Hogan, Kevin Nash, Macho Man, Scott Steiner $50.00

WCW Series 1 1994

Brian Knobs $15.00

Jerry Sags $15.00

Hulk Hogan $17.00+

Jimmy Hart $15.00

Jonny B Bad $15.00

Kevin Sullivan $15.00

Rick Flair (Blue Tights) $17.00+

Rick Flair (Purple Tights) $17,00+

Sting $15.00

Vader $15.00

Series 2

Hulk Hogan $17.00

Jimmy Hart $15.00

Jonny B Bad $15.00

Kevin Sullivan $15.00

Macho Man Randy Savage $17.00+

Rick Flair (Green Tights) $17.00+

Rick Flair (Purple Tights) $17.00+

Sting $15.00

Vader $15.00

Series 3

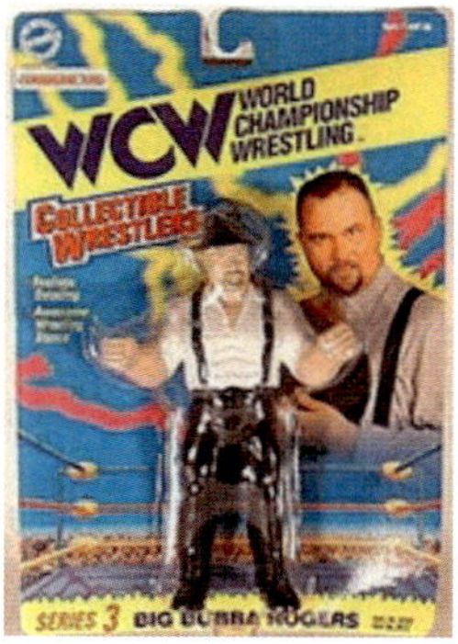

Alex Wright $15.00
Big Bubba Rogers $15.00
Booker T $20.00+
Craig Pittman $15.00
Giant $15.00
Hulk Hogan $15.00
Macho Man Randy Savage $17.00+
Rick Flair (Red Tights) $15.00
Stevie Ray $15.00
Sting (Black Outfit) $15.00

Tag Teams Series 1

Harlem Heat (Black) $70.00+
Hulk Hogan and Sting $25.00
Nasty Boys $25.00
Nasty Boys (In Green) $25.00

Tag Team Series 2

Harlem Heat (Red) $70.00+
Hulk Hogan and Sting $25.00
Nasty Boys (Pink Shirts) $25.00

Tag Teams Series 3

Harlem Heat (Blue) $45.00
Blue Bloods $40.00
Hollywood Hogan and Macho Man $50.00

WCW Monday Nitro Limited Edition Series 1 1997

Booker T $15.00
Hollywood Hogan $15.00
Lex Luger $15.00
Randy Savage $15.00
Rick Flair $15.00
Stevie Ray $15.00
Sting $15.00
Taskmaster $15.00

WCW Monday Nitro Limited Edition Series 2 1997

Brian Knobs $15.00
Jerry Sags $15.00
Giant $15.00

WCW Monday Nitro 1997

Chris Benoit $30.00+
Giant $15.00
Lex Luger $15.00
Sting $15.00
Taskmaster $15.00

WCW Monday Nitro NWO 1997

Hollywood Hogan $20.00
Hollywood Hogan and Denis Rodman $75.00
Kevin Nash $20.00
Scott Hall

WCW Monday Nitro Tag Teams 1997

Lex Luger and Sting $35.00

Scott Hall and Kevin Nash $45.00+

Just Toys 'Bend-Ems'

Item | Value

1990 JusToys - Bend-Ems

Arn Anderson: $8.00
Barry Windham: $7.00
Brian Pillman: $8.00
Butch Reed: $7.00
Lex Luger: $7.00
Ric Flair: $7.00
Rick Steiner: $7.00
Ron Simmons: $7.00
Scott Steiner: $7.00
Sid Vicious: $7.00
Sting: $7.00
Tom Zenk: $7.00

1995-97 Bend-Ems

Ahmed Johnson: $8.00
Bret "Hit Man" Hart: $8.00
British Bulldog: $8.00
Diesel: $8.00
Doink: $8.00
Faarooq: $8.00
Goldust: $8.00
Lex Luger: $8.00
Mabel: $8.00
Mankind: $8.00
Paul Bearer - comes with Superslam! Wrestling ring: $300.00
Ring: $20.00
Razor Ramon: $8.00
Rocky Maivia: $8.00
Shawn Michaels: $8.00
Stone Cold Steve Austin: $10.00
Sunny: $8.00
Sycho Sid: $8.00
Undertaker: $8.00
Vader: $8.00

Wildman Marc Mero: $8.00
Yokozuna: $8.00
1-2-3 Kid: $8.00

Famous Fights 2 Packs 1997
Stone Cold Steve Austin vs. Bret "Hitman" Hart: $15.00
Ahmed Johnson vs. Faarooq: $15.00
Undertaker vs. Mankind: $15.00

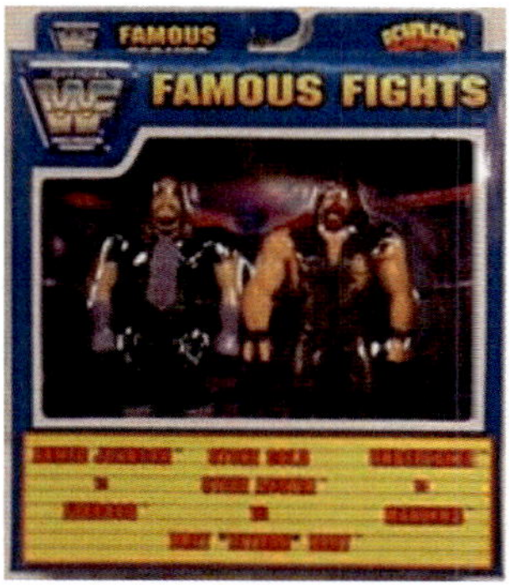

Bend-Ems Rings with Figures
SuperSlam! Wrestling Ring w/ Goldust &
Vader: $30.00
Michaels & S. Austin: $30.00
Undertaker & Hunter Hearst Helmsley: $30.00

Bend-Ems Series 1
Bret hart: $8.00
Doink: $7.00
Lex Luger: $7.00
Razor Ramon: $7.00
Diesel: $7.00

Bend-Ems Series 2
Undertaker: $7.00
British Bulldog: $7.00
1-2-3 Kind: $7.00
Mable: $7.00

Bend-Ems Series 3
Shawn Michaels: $7.00
Goldust: $7.00
Yokozuna: $7.00
Ahmed Johnson: $7.00

Bend-Ems Series 4
Sycho Sid: $7.00
Sunny: $7.00
Marc Mero: $7.00
Vader: $7.00

Bend-Ems Series 5
Rocky Maivia: $7.00
Mankind: $7.00
Faarooq: $7.00
Steve Austin: $7.00

Bend-Ems Series 6
Hawk: $7.00
Animal: $7.00
Undertaker: $7.00
Triple H: $7.00
Powerhouse 7 piece set: $27.00

Bend-Ems Series 7
Owen Hart: $10.00
Crush: $7.00
The Patriot: $7.00
Ken Shamrock: $7.00

Bend-Ems Series 8
Kane: $8.00
Taka Michinoku: $7.00
Chyna: $7.00
Jeff Jarrett: $7.00

Bend-Ems Series 9
X-Pac: $7.00
Cactus Jack: $7.00
Sable: $7.00
Brian Christoper: $7.00

Bend-Ems Series 10
Road Dogg: $7.00
Billy Gunn: $7.00
Steve Blackman: $7.00
Edge: $7.00

Bend-Ems Series 11
Val venis: $7.00
Godfather: $7.00
Vince McMahon: $7.00
Al Snow: $7.00

Bend-Ems Series 12
Big Boss Man: $7.00
Big Show: $7.00
Steve Austin: $7.00
Mankind: $7.00
Undertaker: $7.00

Bend-Ems Series 13
D'Lo Brown: $7.00
Bob Holly: $7.00
Steve Austin: $7.00
Shane McMahon: $7.00
Droz: $7.00

Bend-Ems Series 14
Matt Hardy: $7.00
Jeff Hardy: $7.00
The Rock: $7.00
Chris Jericho: $7.00

Stretch-Ems
Bret "The Hit Man" Hart: $10.00
Lex Luger: $10.00
The Rock: $10.00

Playmates Toy Company Guide

Item | Value

1997 Playmates Ringmasters

Undertaker: $5.00
Shawn Michaels: $5.00
Bret Hart: $5.00
Sycho Sid: $5.00
Goldust: $5.00
Yokozuna: $5.00

Heroes of Wrestling 9 Inch Figures

Sycho Sid: $30.00
Undertaker: $30.00

1997 Grudge Match with Mini Rings

Bret Hart & Steve Austin: $13.00
Yokozuna & Ahmed Johnson: $10.00
Undertaker & Mankind: $20.00+
Shawn Michaels & Owen Hart: $10.00
Sycho Sid & vader: $10.00
Goldust & Savio Vega: $10.00

1997 Playmates Strechin'

Bret Hart: $8.00

Shawn Michaels: $8.00

Undertaker: $8.00

Sycho Sid: $8.00

14 Inch Talking Figures

Undertaker: $30.00

Galoob WCW Figures

Item | Value

1990-1991 WCW US Version

Arn Anderson: $50.00
Barry Windham: $50.00
Big Josh: $150.00
Butch Reed: $50.00
Flyin' Brian Pillman: $50.00
Lex Luger: $50.00
Ric Flair: $50.00
Rick Steiner: $50.00
Ron Simmons: $50.00
Scott Steiner: $50.00
Sid Vicious: $50.00
Sting: $50.00
Z-man Tom Zenk: $50.00

1990-1991 US Verison Tag Team

Arn Anderson & Tom Zenk: $50.00
Ric Flair & Arn Anderson: $50.00
The Steiner Brothers: $50.00
Ron Simmons & Butch Reed: $50.00
Sid Vicious & Barry Windham: $50.00
Lex Luger & Sting: $50.00

1991 WCW UK Version

Arn Anderson: $50.00
Barry Windham: $50.00
Ric Flair: $50.00
Butch Reed: $50.00
Sid Vicious: $50.00
Z-Man Tom Zenk: $50.00
Big Josh: $50.00
El Gigante: $50.00
Dustin Rhodes: $50.00

Brian Pillman: $50.00
Lex Luger: $50.00
Sting: $50.00

WCW 14 Figures

Lex Luger: $57.00
Ric Flair: $75.00
Sid Vicious: $55.00
Sting: $60.00

1991 Galoob - 5" Figures

Jimmy Garvin: $60.00
Michael P.S. Hayes: $60.00
Scott Steiner (pink & black tights): $50.00
Sting (red tights): $50.00

Toy Biz WCW

Item | Value

1999 WCW 6 Inch figures Smash n' Slam

Diamond Dallas Page: $7.00
Goldberg: $7.00
Kevin Nash: $7.00
Scott Hall: $7.00
Hollywood Hogan: $7.00
Macho Man Randy Savage: $7.00
Sting: $7.00
Lex Luger: $7.00
Giant

1999 WCW 6 Inch figures Smash n' Slam 2 packs

Sting & Hollywood Hogan: $10.00
Giant & Kevin Nash: $10.00
Macho Man Randy Savage & Elizabeth: $10.00

2001 WCW 6 inch figure Bruisers

Bam Bam Bigalow: $7.00
Stevie Ray: $7.00
Billy Kidman: $7.00
Diamond Dallas Page: $7.00
Disco Inferno: $7.00
Goldberg: $7.00
Macho Man Randy Savage: $7.00
Raven: $9.00
Sting: $7.00
Rey Mysterio: $10.00
Kevin Nash: $7.00
Wrath: $7.00

2001 Superstars 4 Pack (in white mail order box)

llywood Hogan, Goldberg, Sting & Diamond Dallas Page: $27.00

2001 WCW 6 Inch figures Ring Fighters

Chris Benoit: $14.00+
Bret hart: $15.00+
Goldberg: $7.00
Sting: $7.00
Scott Steiner: $10.00
Booker T: $12.00

2001 WCW Slam n' Crunch

Perry Saturn: $10.00
Buff Bagwell: $7.00
Goldberg: $7.00
Sting: $7.00
Konnan: $7.00
Kevin Nash: $7.00

2001 Slam Force

Sting: $7.00
Goldberg: $7.00
Kevin Nah: $7.00
Bret Hart: $9.00
Chris Benoit: $12.00
Hollywood Hogan: $9.00

2001 WCW Toy Biz Power Slam Series 1
Dennis Rodman: $17.00
Hulk Hogan: $7.00
Hak: $7.00
Sid Vicious: $9.00
Goldberg: $7.00

WCW Slam Series 2
Buff Bagwell: $7.00
Roddy Piper: $10.00
Sting: $7.00
Kevin Nash: $9.00
Kanyon: $7.00

2001 Thunder Slam
Sting & bret Hart: $17.00
Scott Hall & Kevin Nash: $15.00
Goldberg & Bam Bam Bigalow: $12.00

Grip'n Flip Series 1
Chris Jericho & Dean Malenko: $22.00
Raven & Diamond Dallas Page: $15.00
Goldberg & Hollywood Hogan: $15.00

2001 Ring Masters
Lex Luger: $7.00
Bret Hart: $17.00
Goldberg: $10.00
Rick Steiner: $7.00
Chris Jericho: $12.00
Hollywood Hogan: $12.00

WCW TNT
Goldberg: $7.00
Vampiro: $10.00
Jeff Jarrett: $7.00
Scott Steiner: $9.00

WCW Bash at the Beach
Bret Hart: $7.00
Sting: $10.00
Goldberg: $7.00
Lex Luger: $9.00
Diamond Dallas Page: $7.00

WCW Toy Biz Unleashed
Shane Douglas: $7.00
Billy Kidman: $10.00
Mike Awesome: $7.00
Vampiro: $10.00
Hollywood Hogan & Ric Flair: $14.00
Goldberg & Sycho Sid: $9.00
Sting & Lex Luger: $7.00

WCW Toy Biz Gross Out Wrestlers

Goldberg: $7.00
Sid Vicious: $10.00
Sting: $7.00
Jeff Jarrett: $7.00
Buff Bagwell: $7.00
Kevin Nash: $10.00
Goldberg: $7.00
Sting: $10.00
Bret Hart: $14.00
Sid: $9.00
Vampiro: $7.00

Battler Arm

Bret Hart: $17.00
Sting: $14.00
Goldberg: $14.00

WCW Bend n' Flex

Sting: $7.00
Scott Steiner: $8.00
Diamond Dallas Page: $7.00
Bret Hart: $10.00
Kevin Nash: $7.00
Goldberg: $7.00
Booker T: $8.00
Scott Hall: $7.00

WCW Bend n' Flex Boxed Sets

Sting, Scott Steiner, Diamond Dallas Page, Bret Hart: $30.00

Goldberg, Booker T, Scott Hall, Kevin Nasg: $30.00

WCW Tuff Talking Series 1

Goldberg & Kevin Nash: $25.00

Sting & Diamond Dallas Page: $25.00

WCW Brawlin' Bikers

Goldberg: $15.00

Diamond Dallas Page: $15.00

Sting: $15.00

WCW Tuff Talking Series 2

Macho Man Randy Savage: $15.00

Buff Bagwell: $15.00

Konnan: $15.00

Scott Steiner: $15.00

Bashin' Brawlers 21 inch Figures

Goldberg: $20.00

Diamond Dallas Page: $25.00

Bret Hart: $25.00+

Scott Steiner: $25.00

Sting: $20.00

Kevin Nash: $25.00

Boxed Sets and Rings

IV Horsemen: $100.00+

Announcer #1: $20.00

The Evolution of Sting: $27.00

Nitro Arena with Entrance Way: $20.00

Bash at the Beach Ring: $20.00

Ladder Accessory Pack: $20.00

Smash N' Slam Ring: $20.00

Smash N' Slam Ring (eith Gene Okerlund): $20.00

Superbrawl 2000 Ring: $18.00

Announcer #2: $20.00

Heavyweight Championship: $23.00

Red & Black Attack (shirt editon): $37.00

Slamboree 2000 Ring: $20.00

New Japan Pro Wrestling

Item | Value

1998-2002 New Japan Pro wrestling

Riki Chosyu: $30.00
Masahiro Chono: $21.00
The Great Muta: $37.00+
Kenuke Sasaki: $25.00
El Samurai: $25.00
Takashi Lizuka: $25.00
Antonio Inoki (Bronze with Belt): $20.00
Seiji Sakagushi: $15.00
Yugi Nagata: $15.00
Kenji Mutoh: $25.00+
Masahire Saitho (bronze): $20.00
Antonio Inoki (bronze with robe): $21.00
Tatasutoshi Gotoh: $15.00
Tsuyoshi Kosaka: $15.00
Akira Maeda: $15.00
Justing thunder Lyger #2: $35.00+
Tasuhito Takaiwa: $20.00
Antonio Inoki (shirt & tie): $15.00
Yoshiaki Fujiwara: $15.00
Jumbo Tsuruta: $15.00
Yoshihisa Yamamoto: $20.00
Antonio Inoki (yellow trunks 30th anniv): $21.00
Antonio Inoki (homeless): $15.00
Justing Thunder Lyger #3: $35.00+
Antonio Inoki #1: $15.00
Antonio Inoki #2: $15.00
Minoru Tanaka: $20.00
Shinya Hashimoto: $15.00
Takashi Lizuka: $21.00
Jinsei Shinzaki: $15.00
Kengo Watanabe: $20.00
Akira Maeda: $15.00
Tadao Yasuda: $15.00

Hidekazu Tanaka: $15.00
Michiyoshi Ohara: $20.00
Justin Thuder Lyger #1: $21.00+
Kazuno Yamazaki: $15.00
Masahire Chono: $15.00
Jinsei Shinzaki #2: $15.00
Rickson Gracie: $15.00
Junji Hirata: $20.00
Osamu Kide: $15.00
Tasumi Fujinami: $15.00
Kohji Kanemoto: $15.00
Shinjiro Ohani: $20.00
Hiroshi Hase #2: $15.00
Kendoh Ka-Shin: $15.00
Ryuishi Takaiwa: $15.00
The Great Muta: $30.00+
The Great Muta #2: $27.00
The Great Muta #3: $27.00
Ensen Inoue: $20.00
Ryuichi Takaiwa: $20.00
Masakatsu Funaki: $15.00
Hiroyoshi Tenzan: $15.00
Manabu Nakanishi: $15.00
Kiyoshi Tamura: $20.00
Satoshi Kojima: $21.00
Osamu Tanka: $15.00
Naoya Ogawa: $15.00
Atasushi Ohnita: $15.00
Hiroshi Hase #1: $15.00
Masa Saitoh: $20.00
Hayabusa #1: $15.00
Hayabusa #2: $15.00
Kazuyuki Fulita: $15.00

1998-2002 2 Figure Pack

Inoki & Gotch: $27.00
Break Bunny (2 girl pack): $30.00
Giant & Silva: $25.00
Yoshiro Takayama & Takao Omori: $26.00
Akira Taue & Jun Akiyama: $27.00

1998-2002 Delux Figures

The Great Muta #1: $45.00+
The Great Muta #2: $45.00+
Mil Mascaras (silver mask): $25.00
Mil Mascaras (black mask): $25.00
Justin Thunder Lyger: $50.00+
Don Frye (with UFC belt): $40.00
Power Warrior: $25.00
Muta & Chono: $47.00
Tatsumi Fujinami: $25.00+
The Great Nita: $25.00
Jinsei Shinzakai: $37.00
Referee Tiger Hattori: $25.00
Hakushi: $25.00

2002 4 inch Figures

The Great Muta: $10.00
Keiji Mutoh: $7.00
Riki Chosyo: $7.00
masahiro Chono (with Glasses): $8.00
Masahiro Chono (without Glasses): $7.00

Miscellenous

War Promotion:
Takada Nobuiko: $8.00
Genichiro Tenryn: $7.00
Rickson Gracie: $7.00
Masakatsu Funaki: $8.00

All Japan Series 1:
Misawa: $17.00
Kobashi: $25.00+
Akiyama: $20.00
Kawada: $20.00
Taue: $20.00
Baba: $19.00

All Japan Series 2:
Stan Hansen: $23.00
Giant Baba: $20.00
Vader: $22.00
Gary Albright: $18.00
Johnny Ace: $20.00
Ogawa: $20.00
Kimura: $19.00

FMW Wrestling:
Hayabusa (red): $20.00
Hayabusa (blue): $20.00
Hayabusa (black): $20.00
Hayabusa (white): $20.00

AWA Remco/AAA/Lucha Libre/Magnificent

1985-1986 AWA Remco
Figure | Price

1985 AWA Series 1 (Tag Teams)
Fabulous Freebirds (3): $245.00
Fabulous Ones: $200.00
Gagne's Raiders: $210.00
High Flyers: $210.00
Long Riders: $200.00
Road Warriors: $220.00
Road Warriors w/ Manager: $290.00

1985 AWA Series 2 (Tag Teams)
Greg Gagne & Curt Henning: $180.00
"Wild" Bill Irwin & Scott "Hog" Irwin: $180.00
Michael Hayes, Terry Gordy & Buddy Roberts $200.00
Jimmy Garvin, Steve Regel & Precious: $200.00
Hawk, Animal & Paul Ellering: $290.00

1986 AWA Series 3 (Grudge Series)
Abdullah & Carlos Colon: $210.00
Scott Hall & Jimmy Garvin: $200.00
Nick Bockwinkle & Larry Zbyszko: $200.00
Jerry Blackwell & Stan Hansen: $210.00

1986 AWA Series 4 (Mat Mania)

Boris Zuchov: $250.00
Buddy Rose: $220.00
Doug Somers: $220.00
Nord the Barbarian: $240.00
Sheik Adnan: $250.00
Referee with Brown Hair and Referee with Grey Hair: $210.00 each
Shawn Michaels: $340.00
Marty Janetty: $220.00

1985-1986 AWA Remco Accessories

Steel cage match playset: $500.00
AWA Remco Belt: $200.00
AWA Remco Ring: $200.00

AWA Battle Royal Gift Set Series 1

Road Warriors: $120.00
Fabulous Ones: $120.00
Baron Von Raschke: $120.00
Rick Martel: $120.00
Referee: $120.00

AWA 2-packs - Grudge Matches

Colon & Abdullah: $110.00
Hall & Garvin: $100.00
Hansen & Blackwell: $100.00
Zbyszko & Bockwinkle: $110.00

AWA Main Events
Flair & Zbyszko: $100.00
Von Raschnke & Martel: $65.00

AWA Thumbsters
Animal: $30.00
Greg Gagne: $30.00
Hawk: $30.00
Larry Zbyszko: $30.00
Ric Flair: $30.00
Rick Martel: $30.00

AAA by Kelian
Octagon: $20.00
Konna: $17.00
Hijo del Santo: $20.00
Rey Mysterio Jr: $22.00
Fuerza Guerrera: $20.00
La Parka: $20.00
Heavy Metal: $20.00
Perro Aguayo: $20.00
Psicosis: $18.00
Blue Panther: $20.00
Cien Caras: $20.00
Mascara Sagrada: $20.00

1992 Original Sanfransico Toy Makers CMLL Lucha Libre Luchadores

Destructor I: $60.00
Destructor I & II: $60.00
Dos Caras: $60.00
Dr.Wagner: $60.00
Espertro jr: $60.00
Felino: $60.00
Fishman: $60.00
Fuerza Maya: $60.00
Fuerza Guerrera: $60.00
Hijo Dialo: $60.00
Huracan Ramirez: $60.00
Ice Killer: $60.00
Jushin Lyger: $60.00
Juventud Guerrera: $60.00
Kendo Star: $60.00
Konnan: $60.00
Kung Fu: $60.00
La Parka: $60.00
Las Chivas: $60.00
Lizmark: $60.00
Love Machine: $60.00
Mano Negra: $60.00
Mascara Ano Dos: $60.00
Atlantis: $60.00
Mascara Sagrada: $60.00
Bronce: $60.00
Mil Mascaras 1: $60.00
Mil Mascaras 2: $60.00
Mosco: $60.00
Ninja Turtle: $60.00
Octagon: $60.00
Oro: $60.00
Pentera: $60.00
Payaso Amarillo: $60.00
Payaso Roja: $60.00

Pegasus Kid: $60.00
Tigre Blanco: $60.00
Picudo: $60.00
Pierroth: $60.00
Pirata Morgan: $60.00
Plata: $60.00
Psicosis: $60.00
Rayo de Jalisco: $60.00
Rey Mysterio Jr: $60.00
Blue Panther: $60.00
Sangre Azteca: $60.00
Santo Jr: $60.00
Shufu Guerrera: $60.00
Solar: $60.00
Volador: $60.00
Sombre De Plata: $60.00
Super Astro: $60.00
Super Menuco: $60.00
Talisman: $60.00
Blue Demon: $60.00
Tinisblas: $60.00
Ultimo Dragon: $150.00
Vampiro: $60.00
Vilano: $60.00
Aguila Solitaro: $60.00
Canek (green): $60.00
Kahoz: $60.00
La Calaca: $60.00
Angel Blanco: $66.00
Cien Caras: $60.00
Super Calo: $60.00
Abismo Negro: $60.00
Matematico: $60.00
Mascara Maligna: $60.00
Perro Aguayo: $60.00
Ricky Marvin: $60.00
Solitario: $60.00

Lucha Libre 10 inch Figures

Latin Lover: $22.00
Maniaco: $15.00
Charlie Manson: $16.00
Histeria: $17.00
Misterioso: $20.00
Mosco: $18.00
Abismo Negro 1: $20.00
Espertro Jr: $17.00
Perro Aguayo: $20.00
Blue Demon: $15.00
Cibernetico 1: $15.00
Felino: $17.00
El Samurai: $20.00
Octagon: $20.00
Payosos: $18.00
Psicosis: $22.00+
Psicosis AAA: $25.00+
Canek: $20.00
Mascara Sagrada Jr: $22.00
Tineblas Solitario: $20.00
Ultimo Dragon: $27.00+
Kendoh Ka Shin: $20.00
La Parka: $20.00

Magnificent Wrestler

Mano Negra: $22.00
Angel Blaco: $20.00
Pierroth: $20.00
Ultimo Dragon: $24.00+
Hurrican Ramirez: $20.00
Konna: $18.00
Mil Mascaras: $20.00
Misterioso: $20.00
Octagon: $20.00
El Mexicano: $20.00
Ray De Jalisco: $20.00
Rey Mysterio Jr: $24.00+

Solar: $20.00
Blue Panther: $18.00
Universo 2000: $20.00
Villiano: $20.00
Atlantis: $20.00

Jesse Ventura Little Big Head Figures
Jesse Ventura (Navy Seal): $32.00
Jesse Ventura (Football Coach): $33.00
Jesse Ventura (Governor): $34.00

Jesse Ventura 12 inch Dolls
Jesse Ventura (Navy Seal): $18.00
Jesse Ventura (Football Coach): $15.00
Jesse Ventura (Governor): $15.00

Bobbin' Heads
Diamond Dallas Page: $15.00
Goldberg: $15.00
Hollywood Hogan: $20.00
Sting: $17.00

1992 - WWF Mini Wrestlers

Natural Disasters & LOD: $55.00

Beefcake, Bushwackers & Valentine: $55.00

Perfect, Duggan, Piper & Tornado: $55.00

Royal Rumble Ring (with 6 figures): $55.00

2015 Funko WWE Mystery Minis Checklist

Andre the Giant: $30.00

Brie Bella: $20.00

Nikki Bella: $20.00

Daniel Bryan: $50.00

John Cena: $20.00

Ric FlairHulk Hogan: $30.00

The Iron Sheik: $20.00

The Rock: $25.00

George "The Animal" Steele: $20.00

The Undertaker: $30.00

The Ultimate Warrior: $30.00

Funko Pop WWE Figures complete set and entire series

Estimated release date is shown below when available.

01 John Cena: $20.00

01 John Cena Black Shorts - WWE Events: $20.00

01 John Cena Green - WWE.com: $20.00

01 John Cena The U Hat: $20.00

02 CM Punk: $50.00

02 CM Punk Pink Trunks - Hot Topics: $120.00

03 The Rock: $20.00

04 Sheamus: $20.00

05 Stone Cold Steve Austin: $20.00

05 Stone Cold Steve Austin 2k16: $20.00

06 Rey Mysterio: $50.00

06 Rey Mysterio Teal Pink - 7-11: $100.00

06 Rey Mysterio Black Mask - 2014: $50.00

07 Daniel Bryan Series 2: $20.00

07 Daniel Bryan Red Trunks - Hot Topic: $20.00

08 Undertaker: $20.00

09 Triple H: $20.00

10 Macho Man Randy Savage: $20.00

10 Macho Man Randy Savage Pink Bandana: $50.00

10 Macho Man Randy Savage Purple Trunks - FYE: $50.00

11 Hulk Hogan: $20.00

11 Hulk Hogan "Hulk Rules" Shirt: $20.00

12 AJ Lee Series3: $20.00

13 Brock Lesnar - Walmart: $20.00

14 Brie Bella: $20.00

15 Nikki Bella: $20.00

16 Paige: $20.00

17 Ric Flair - Target: $20.00

18 Rowdy Roddy Piper - Target: $25.00

19 Sting: $20.00

19 Wolfpack Sting: $25.00

20 Ultimate Warrior: $20.00

21 Andre The Giant: $20.00

23 Roman Reigns: $30.00

24 Seth Rollins: $20.00

25 Bret Hart: $20.00

26 Eva Marie: $20.00

27 Kevin Owens: $20.00

28 Bray Wyatt: $20.00

Other Figures: $20.00

Bella Twins Red - WWE Events: $20.00

Bella Twins Black: $20.00

The New Day 3-Pack: $20.00

Freddy Funko #34 Hulk Hogan - 2015 SDCC: $150.00

Freddy Funko #52 Sting - 2016 SDCC: $150.00

2015-2016 Funko WWE Series 3

12 AJ Lee: $20.00

13 Brock Lesnar (Wal-Mart): $100.00+

14 Brie Bella: $20.00

15 Nikki Bella: $30.00

16 Paige - 2/2106: $20.00

17 Ric Flair (Target): $35.00

19 Sting: $35.00

20 Ultimate Warrior - 2/2016: $30.00

21 Andre The Giant: $35.00

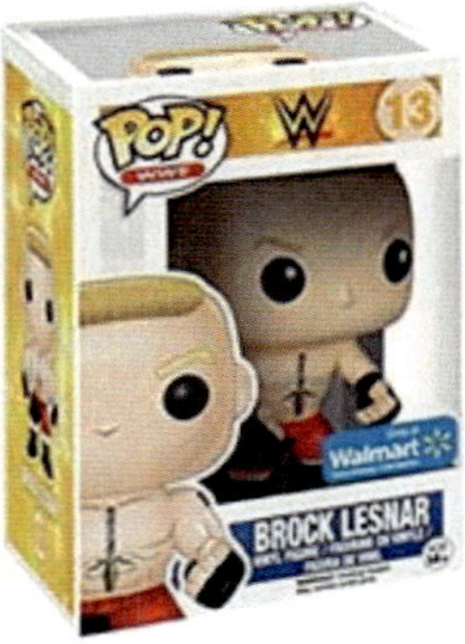

2014 Funko Pop WWE Series 2

07 Daniel Bryan: $30.00

08 Undertaker: $35.00

09 Triple H: $30.00

10 "Macho Man" Randy Savage: $30.00

11 Hulk Hogan: $30.00

Best of 2010 - WWE Elite Collection (Mattel)

John Cena WWE Elite Collection - Best of 2010 Released in 2011: $20.00

Kane WWE Elite Collection - Best of 2010 Released in 2011 by: $20.00

Randy Orton WWE Elite Collection - Best of 2010 Released in 2011: $20.00

Rey Mysterio WWE Elite Collection - Best of 2010: $30.00

Triple HWWE Elite Collection - Best of 2010 Released in 2011: $20.00

Undertaker WWE Elite Collection - Best of 2010 Released in 2011: $20.00

Best of 2011 - WWE Elite Collection (Mattel)

John Cena WWE Elite Collection - Best of 2011 Released in 2012: $20.00

John Morrison WWE Elite Collection - Best of 2011 Released in 2012: $20.00

Randy Orton WWE Elite Collection - Best of 2011 Released in 2012: $20.00

Rey Mysterio WWE Elite Collection - Best of 2011 Released in 2012: $20.00

Sheamus WWE Elite Collection - Best of 2011 Released in 2012: $20.00

Best of Pay-Per-View 2011 - WWE Elite Collection (Mattel)

Big Show (Wrestlemania 28) WWE Elite Released in 2012: $20.00

CM Punk (Wrestlemania 28) WWE Elite Released in 2012: $20.00

Ricardo Rodriguez [Build a Figure] WWE Elite Released in 2012: $20.00

Shawn Michaels (Wrestlemania 28) WWE Elite Released in 2012: $20.00

The Miz (Wrestlemania 28) WWE Elite Released in 2012: $20.00

Best of Pay-Per-View 2012 - WWE Elite Collection (Mattel)

Christian (No Way Out) WWE Elite Collection - 2012: $20.00

John Cena (Extreme Rules) WWE Elite Collection - 2012: $20.00

John Laurinaitis [Build a Figure] WWE Elite Collection 2012: $20.00

Sheamus (Money in the Bank) WWE Elite Collection 2012: $20.00

Sin Cara (No Way Out) WWE Elite Collection 2012: $20.00

Best of Pay-Per-View 2013 - WWE Elite Collection (Mattel)

Brock Lesnar (Wrestlemania 29) WWE Elite Collection 2013: $75.00+

CM Punk (Wrestlemania 29) WWE Elite Collection 2013: $35.00

Daniel Bryan (Wrestlemania 29) WWE Elite Collection 2013: $20.00

John Cena (Wrestlemania 29) WWE Elite Collection 2013: $20.00

Paul Heyman [Build a Figure] WWE Elite Collection 2013: $20.00

Exclusives - WWE Elite Collection Mattel

Triple H (Wrestlemania 29) (Toys R Us) WWE 2013: $40.00

Series 1 - WWE Elite Collection Mattel

CM Punk WWE Elite Collection - Series 1 Released in 2010: $40.00+

Edge WWE Elite Collection - Series 1 Released in 2010: $20.00

MVP WWE Elite Collection - Series 1 Released in 2010: $20.00

Rey Mysterio WWE Elite Collection - Series 1 Released in 2010: $35.00

Undertaker WWE Elite Collection - Series 1 Released in 2010: $30.00

Series 2 - WWE Elite Collection (Mattel)

Batista WWE Elite Collection - Series 2 Released in 2010: $20.00

Matt Hardy WWE Elite Collection - Series 2 Released in 2010: $20.00

R-Truth WWE Elite Collection - Series 2 Released in 2010: $20.00

Randy Orton WWE Elite Collection - Series 2 Released in 2010: $20.00

Ted DiBiase WWE Elite Collection - Series 2 Released im 2010: $20.00

Triple H WWE Elite Collection - Series 2 Released in 2010: $20.00

Triple H (Bottle Packaging) WWE Elite Collection - Series 2 Released in 2010: $35.00

Series 3 - WWE Elite Collection (Mattel)

Christian WWE Elite Collection - Series 3 Released in 2010: $20.00

Cody Rhodes WWE Elite Collection - Series 3 Released in 2010: $20.00

John Cena WWE Elite Collection - Series 3 Released in 2010: $20.00

Santino Marella WWE Elite Collection - Series 3 Released in 2010: $20.00

Shawn Michaels WWE Elite Collection - Series 3 Released in 2010: $20.00

The Miz WWE Elite Collection - Series 3 Released in 2010: $20.00

Series 4 - WWE Elite Collection (Mattel)

Big Show WWE Elite Collection - Series 4 Released in 2010: $20.00

Chris Jericho (Blue Gear) WWE Elite Collection - Series 4 Released in 2010: $30.00

Chris Jericho (Purple Gear) WWE Elite Collection - Series 4 Released in 2010: $30.00

Finlay WWE Elite Collection - Series 4 Released in 2010: $20.00

John Morrison (Bright Red Robe) - Series 4 Released in 2010 `: $40.00

John Morrison (Dark Red Robe) Series 4 Released in 2010: $40.00

Kane WWE Elite Collection - Series 4 Released in 2010: $20.00

Kofi Kingston WWE Elite Collection - Series 4 Released in 2010: $20.00

Series 5 - WWE Elite Collection (Mattel)

Chavo GuerreroWWE Elite Collection - Series 5 Released in 2010: $20.00

Dolph Ziggler WWE Elite Collection - Series 5 Released in 2010: $20.00

Jack Swagger no singlet WWE Elite Collection - Series 5 Released in 2010: $20.00

Jack Swagger (Singlet) WWE Elite Collection - Series 5 Released in 2010: $20.00

Mark Henry WWE Elite Collection - Series 5 Released in 2010: $20.00

Rey Mysterio WWE Elite Collection - Series 5 Released in 2010: $40.00

Vladimir Kozlov (No Detail on Jacket Sleeves) WWE Elite 2010: $30.00

Vladimir Kozlov (With Detail on Jacket Sleeves) WWE Elite 2010: $30.00

Series 6 - WWE Elite Collection (Mattel)

Batista WWE Elite Collection - Series 6 Released in 2010: $20.00

CM Punk WWE Elite Collection - Series 6 Released in 2010: $40.00+

Goldust WWE Elite Collection - Series 6 Released in 2010: $20.00

JTG WWE Elite Collection - Series 6 Released in 2010: $20.00

Matt Hardy WWE Elite Collection - Series 6 Released in 2010: $20.00

Shad WWE Elite Collection - Series 6 Released in 2010: $20.00

Series 7 - WWE Elite Collection (Mattel)

David Hart Smith WWE Elite Collection - Series 7 Released in 2011: $50.00+

Hornswoggle WWE Elite Collection - Series 7 Released in 2011: $20.00

John Cena WWE Elite Collection - Series 7 Released in 2011: $20.00

Shawn Michaels WWE Elite Collection - Series 7 Released in 2011: $30.00

Triple HWWE Elite Collection - Series 7 Released in 2011: $30.00

Tyson Kidd WWE Elite Collection - Series 7 Released in 2011: $30.00+

Series 8 - WWE Elite Collection

Series 8 - WWE Elite Collection (Mattel) Checklist Drew McIntyre: $20.00

Steven Reagal WWE Elite Released in 2011 by Matt: $20.00

EdgeWWE Elite Collection - Series 8 Released in 2011: $20.00

Evan BourneWWE Elite Collection - Series 8 Released in 2011: $20.00

Sheamus WWE Elite Collection - Series 8 Released in 2011: $20.00

UndertakerWWE Elite Collection - Series 8 Released in 2011: $20.00

Series 9 - WWE Elite Collection (Mattel) 2011

Kofi KingstonWWE Elite Collection - Series 9: $10.00

Luke GallowsWWE Elite Collection - Series 9: $10.00

MVPWWE Elite Collection - Series 9: $10.00

Randy OrtonWWE Elite Collection - Series 9: $10.00

The MizWWE Elite Collection - Series 9: $20.00

Zack RyderWWE Elite Collection - Series 9: $20.00

Series 10 - WWE Elite Collection (Mattel) 2011

Big ShowWWE Elite Collection - Series 10: $20.00

KaneWWE Elite Collection - Series 10: $20.00

Ted DiBiaseWWE Elite Collection - Series 10: $20.00

John MorrisonWWE Elite Collection - Series 10: $20.00

R-TruthWWE Elite Collection - Series 10: $20.00

Yoshi TatsuWWE Elite Collection - Series 10: $20.00

Series 11 - WWE Elite Collection (Mattel) 2011

ChristianWWE Elite Collection - Series 11: $20.00

John CenaWWE Elite Collection - Series 11: $20.00

The MizWWE Elite Collection - Series 11: $20.00

CM PunkWWE Elite Collection - Series 11: $40.00+

Wade BarrettWWE Elite Collection - Series 11: $20.00

Rey Mysterio WWE Elite Collection - Series 11: $40.00

Series 12 - WWE Elite Collection (Mattel)

Alberto Del RioWWE Elite Collection - Series 12: $20.00

Justin Gabriel WWE Elite Collection - Series 12: $10.00

Papa Shango (Flashback) WWE Elite Collection - Series 12: $20.00

Daniel BryanWWE Elite Collection - Series 12: $20.00

Kane (Flashback) WWE Elite Collection - Series 12: $20.00

Randy Orton WWE Elite Collection - Series 12: $20.00

Series 13 - WWE Elite Collection (Mattel) 2012

Big ShowWWE Elite Collection - Series 13: $20.00

Dolph ZigglerWWE Elite Collection - Series 13: $20.00

Rey MysterioWWE Elite Collection - Series 13: $30.00

Cody RhodesWWE Elite Collection - Series 13: $20.00

Edge (Flashback) WWE Elite Collection - Series 13: $30.00

SheamusWWE Elite Collection - Series 13: $10.00

Series 14 - WWE Elite Collection (Mattel) 2012

Alberto Del RioWWE Elite Collection - Series 14: $10.00
Booker T WWE Elite Collection - Series 14: $75.00
The Rock WWE Elite Collection - Series 14: $17.00
Big Bossman WWE Elite Collection - Series 14: $20.00
John Cena WWE Elite Collection - Series 14: $20.00
Undertaker WWE Elite Collection - Series 14: $20.00

Series 15 - WWE Elite Collection (Mattel)

Evan Bourne WWE Elite Collection - Series 15: $10.00
R-Truth WWE Elite Collection - Series 15: $50.00
Sin CaraWWE Elite Collection - Series 15: $10.00
Mark Henry WWE Elite Collection - Series 15: $10.00
Rey Mysterio WWE Elite Collection - Series 15: $25.00
Yokozuna (Flashback) WWE Elite Collection - Series 15: $75.00

Series 16 - WWE Elite Collection (Mattel) 2012

CM Punk WWE Elite Collection - Series 16: $30.00
Ezekiel JacksonWWE Elite Collection - Series 16: $20.00
Kevin Nash (Flashback) WWE Elite Collection - Series 16: $75.00+
The Rock WWE Elite Collection - Series 16: $15.00
Diesel (Flashback) WWE Elite Collection - Series 16: $75.00+
Heath SlaterWWE Elite Collection - Series 16: $10.00
Randy OrtonWWE Elite Collection - Series 16: $20.00

Series 17 - WWE Elite Collection (Mattel) 2012

John Cena WWE Elite Collection - Series 17: $20.00
Kofi Kingston WWE Elite Collection - Series 17: $20.00
Sheamus WWE Elite Collection - Series 17: $20.00
Kelly Kelly WWE Elite Collection - Series 17: $40.00
Mankind WWE Elite Collection - Series 17: $50.00
Zack RyderWWE Elite Collection - Series 17: $10.00

Series 18 - WWE Elite Collection (Mattel) 2012

Brodus Clay WWE Elite Collection - Series 18: $10.00

Rey Mysterio WWE Elite Collection - Series 18: $25.00

Undertaker (Flashback) WWE Elite Collection - Series 18: $35.00+

Jerry Lawler WWE Elite Collection - Series 18: $10.00

Sin Cara WWE Elite Collection - Series 18: $10.00

Wade Barrett WWE Elite Collection - Series 18: $10.00

Series 19 - WWE Elite Collection (Mattel) 2013

Brock Lesnar WWE Elite Collection - Series 19: $70.00+

Dolph Ziggler WWE Elite Collection - Series 19: $10.00

Miss Elizabeth WWE Elite Collection - Series 19: $50.00+

Daniel Bryan WWE Elite Collection - Series 19: $50.00

Kane WWE Elite Collection - Series 19: $20.00

Shawn MichaelsWWE Elite Collection - Series 19: $30.00

Series 20 - WWE Elite Collection (Mattel) 2013

Chris Jericho WWE Elite Collection - Series 20: $20.00

CM Punk WWE Elite Collection - Series 20: $20.00

John CenaWWE Elite Collection - Series 20: $20.00

Christian (Flashback) WWE Elite Collection - Series 20: $25.00+

Cody Rhodes WWE Elite Collection - Series 20: $20.00

Santino MarellaWWE Elite Collection - Series 20: $30.00+

Series 21 - WWE Elite Collection (Mattel) 2013

AJ Lee WWE Elite Collection - Series 21: $10.00

Honky Tonk ManWWE Elite Collection - Series 21: $25.00

Rey Mysterio WWE Elite Collection - Series 21: $20.00

Alberto Del RioWWE Elite Collection - Series 21: $20.00

Randy OrtonWWE Elite Collection - Series 21: $20.00

RybackWWE Elite Collection - Series 21: $10.00

Series 22 - WWE Elite Collection (Mattel) 2013

Big Show WWE Elite Collection - Series 22: $20.00

Kane WWE Elite Collection - Series 22: $20.00

The GiantWWE Elite Collection - Series 22: $10.00

Damien Sandow WWE Elite Collection - Series 22: $10.00

Tensai WWE Elite Collection - Series 22: $10.00

The RockWWE Elite Collection - Series 22: $20.00

Series 23 - WWE Elite Collection (Mattel) 2013

Antonio CesaroWWE Elite Collection - Series 23: $20.00

John CenaWWE Elite Collection - Series 23: $20.00

Triple H (Flashback) WWE Elite Collection - Series 23: $75.00+

JBL (Flashback) WWE Elite Collection - Series 23: $50.00+

Macho Man Randy SavageWWE Elite Collection - Series 23: $50.00+

UndertakerWWE Elite Collection - Series 23: $50.00+

Series 24 - WWE Elite Collection (Mattel)

Dolph ZigglerWWE Elite Collection - Series 24: $20.00

RybackWWE Elite Collection - Series 24: $10.00

Trish StratusWWE Elite Collection - Series 24: $50.00+

Rey MysterioWWE Elite Collection - Series 24: $25.00

The MizWWE Elite Collection - Series 24: $30.00

Wade BarrettWWE Elite Collection - Series 24: $20.00

Series 25 - WWE Elite Collection (Mattel) 2013

Brodus ClayWWE Elite Collection - Series 25: $20.00

Dean AmbroseWWE Elite Collection - Series 25: $10.00

SheamusWWE Elite Collection - Series 25: $20.00

Bruno SammartinoWWE Elite Collection - Series 25: $40.00

Sin CaraWWE Elite Collection - Series 25: $10.00

Seth Rollins WWE Elite Collection - Series 25: $25.00

Series 26 - WWE Elite Collection (Mattel) 2014

Big E LangstonWWE Elite Collection - Series 26: $20.00

Mark HenryWWE Elite Collection - Series 26: $20.00

Roman Reigns (The Shield) WWE Elite Collection - Series 26: $20.00

Jack SwaggerWWE Elite Collection - Series 26: $10.00

Road DoggWWE Elite Collection - Series 26: $15.00

Ultimate Warrior (Flashback) WWE Elite Collection - Series 26: $75.00+

Series 27 - WWE Elite Collection (Mattel) 2014

Billy Gunn (Flashback) WWE Series 27: $25.00

Kofi KingstonWWE Series 27: $10.00

Rikishi (Flashback) WWE (Wearing Entrance Gear) Series 27: $35.00+

FandangoWWE Series 27: $20.00

Rikishi (Flashback) (Entrance Gear on Side) WWE Series 27: $30.00+

Rob Van Dam (RVD) WWE Series 27: $20.00

Series 28 - WWE Elite Collection (Mattel) 2014

Big ShowWWE Elite Collection - Series 28: $10.00

Daniel BryanWWE Elite Collection - Series 28: $20.00

John CenaWWE Elite Collection - Series 28: $10.00

Bray WyattWWE Elite Collection - Series 28: $10.00

Demolition Crush (Flashback) WWE Elite Collection - Series 28: $20.00+

Triple H WWE Elite Collection - Series 28: $15.00

Series 29 - WWE Elite Collection (Mattel) 2014

Andre the GiantWWE Elite Collection - Series 29: $30.00+

Damien SandowWWE Elite Collection - Series 29: $10.00

GoldustWWE Elite Collection - Series 29: $20.00

CM PunkWWE Elite Collection - Series 29: $25.00

Erick RowanWWE Elite Collection - Series 29: $10.00

Luke HarperWWE Elite Collection - Series 29: $20.00

Series 30 - WWE Elite Collection (Mattel) 2014
BatistaWWE Elite Collection - Series 30: $20.00
Lex LugerWWE Elite Collection - Series 30: $20.00
Road Warrior HawkWWE Elite Collection - Series 30: $50.00+
Brock LesnarWWE Elite Collection - Series 30: $75.00+
Road Warrior AnimalWWE Elite Collection - Series 30: $25.00
RybackWWE Elite Collection - Series 30: $10.00

Series 31 - WWE Elite Collection (Mattel) 2014
Dean Ambrose WWE Elite Collection - Series 31: $20.00
Jimmy Uso WWE Elite Collection - Series 31: $10.00
RockWWE Elite Collection - Series 31: $20.00
Jey Uso WWE Elite Collection - Series 31: $20.00
Kane WWE Elite Collection - Series 31: $20.00
Vader WWE Elite Collection - Series 31: $20.00

Series 32 - WWE Elite Collection (Mattel) 2014
Big E Langston WWE Elite Collection - Series 32: $10.00
Daniel BryanWWE Elite Collection - Series 32: $20.00
Rey MysterioWWE Elite Collection - Series 32: $20.00
Cody RhodesWWE Elite Collection - Series 32: $10.00
Mark HenryWWE Elite Collection - Series 32: $10.00
Sin CaraWWE Elite Collection - Series 32: $10.00

Series 33 - WWE Elite Collection (Mattel) 2014
BatistaWWE Elite Collection - Series 33: $10.00
Junkyard DogWWE Elite Collection - Series 33: $25.00+
Seth RollinsWWE Elite Collection - Series 33: $20.00
CesaroWWE Elite Collection - Series 33: $10.00
Roman ReignsWWE Elite Collection - Series 33: $20.00
X-PacWWE Elite Collection - Series 33: $20.00

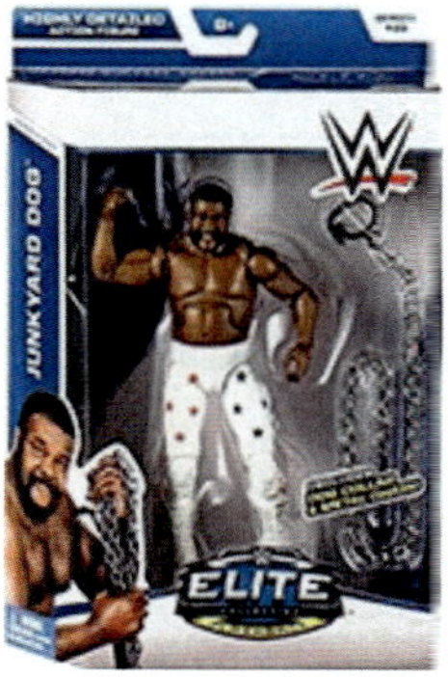

Series 34 - WWE Elite Collection (Mattel) 2015

Bad News BarrettWWE Elite Collection - Series 34: $20.00
Hulk HoganWWE Elite Collection - Series 34: $30.00
PaigeWWE Elite Collection - Series 34: $20.00
Doink the ClownWWE Elite Collection - Series 34: $10.00
John CenaWWE Elite Collection - Series 34: $10.00
RusevWWE Elite Collection - Series 34: $20.00

Series 35 - WWE Elite Collection (Mattel) 2015

DiegoWWE Elite Collection - Series 35: $10.00
Fernando WWE Elite Collection - Series 35: $10.00
Randy OrtonWWE Elite Collection - Series 35: $20.00
EarthquakeWWE Elite Collection - Series 35: $20.00
Luke HarperWWE Elite Collection - Series 35: $10.00
Triple HWWE Elite Collection - Series 35: $20.00

Series 36 - WWE Elite Collection (Mattel)

Bo DallasWWE Elite Collection - Series 36: $20.00
Dean AmbroseWWE Elite Collection - Series 36: $20.00
GoldustWWE Elite Collection - Series 36: $20.00
Bray WyattWWE Elite Collection - Series 36: $20.00
Diamond Dallas PageWWE Elite Collection - Series 36: $20.00
StardustWWE Elite Collection - Series 36: $50.00+

Series 37 - WWE Elite Collection (Mattel) 2015

Brock LesnarWWE Elite Collection - Series 37: $50.00+
Stephanie Mcmahon WWE Elite Collection - Series 37: $20.00
Seth Rollins WWE Elite Collection - Series 37: $20.00
Dean Malenko WWE Elite Collection - Series 37: $50.00
John Cena WWE Elite Collection - Series 37: $25.00
Miz WWE Elite Collection - Series 37: $25.00

Series 38 - WWE Elite Collection (Mattel) 2015

"Macho Man" Randy Savage (Flashback) Series 38: $50.00

Bradshaw (Flashback) WWE Elite Collection - Series 38: $25.00+

Faarooq (Flashback) WWE Elite Collection - Series 38: $25.00 +

Daniel BryanWWE Elite Collection - Series 38: $20.00

Roman ReignsWWE Elite Collection - Series 38: $20.00

Adam Rose WWE Elite Collection - Series 38: $20.00

Series 39 - WWE Elite Collection (Mattel) 2015

Damien MizdowWWE Elite Collection - Series 39: $20.00

Godfather (Flashback) WWE Elite Collection - Series 39: $40.00+

Sycho Sid (Flashback) WWE Elite Collection - Series 39: $40.00+

Sting WWE Elite Collection - Series 39: $30.00

British Bulldog (Flashback) WWE Elite Collection - Series 39: $50.00+

Dolph ZigglerWWE Elite Collection - Series 39: $20.00

Series 40 - WWE Elite Collection (Mattel) 2016

John CenaWWE Elite Collection - Series 40: $20.00

Tyson KiddWWE Elite Collection - Series 40: $40.00+

Irwin R. Schyster (Flashback) WWE Elite Collection - Series 40: $50.00

Sami ZaynWWE Elite Collection - Series 40: $30.00

Umaga (Flashback) WWE Elite Collection - Series 40: $50.00

“Ravishing" Rick Rude (Flashback) - Series 40: $50.00+

Series 41 - WWE Elite Collection (Mattel) 2016

1-2-3 Kid (Flashback) WWE Elite Collection - Series 41: $75.00

Finn BalorWWE Elite Collection - Series 41: $45.00+

RybackWWE Elite Collection - Series 41: $10.00

Dean AmbroseWWE Elite Collection - Series 41: $20.00

LitaWWE Elite Collection - Series 41: $10.00

Terry Funk (Flashback) WWE Elite Collection - Series 41: $50.00

Series 42 - WWE Elite Collection (Mattel) 2016

KalistoWWE Elite Collection - Series 42: $10.00
Nasty Boy Jerry Sags (Flashback) - Series 42: $30.00
Triple H WWE Elite Collection - Series 42: $20.00
Nasty Boy Brian Knobbs (Flashback) Series 42: $30.00
Neville WWE Elite Collection - Series 42: $20.00
Xavier Woods WWE Elite Collection - Series 42: $10.00

Series 43 - WWE Elite Collection (Mattel) 2016

Kofi KingstonWWE Elite Collection - Series 43: $20.00
Samoa JoeWWE Elite Collection - Series 43: $30.00
Bret HartWWE Elite Collection - Series 43: $50.00+
Kevin OwensWWE Elite Collection - Series 43: $20.00
Jim the Anvil Neidhart WWE Elite Collection - Series 43: $50.00+
Alberto Del Rio WWE Elite Collection - Series 43: $10.00

Series 44 - WWE Elite Collection (Mattel) 2016

Big E WWE Elite Collection - Series 44: $20.00
Macho Man Randy Savage - Series 44: $35.00
Sasha Banks - Series 44: $20.00
Sin Cara - Series 44: $20.00
Tugboat - Series 44: $20.00

Series 45 - WWE Elite Collection (Mattel) 2016

Bubba Ray Dudley - WWE Elite Collection (Mattel): $30.00
D-von Dudley - WWE Elite Collection (Mattel): $30.00
Lord Steven Regal - WWE Collection (Mattel): $50.00+
Narcissist Lex Luger - WWE Collection (Mattel): $50.00+
Roman Reigns - WWE Elite Collection: $35.00
Seth Rollins - WWE Elite Collection: $35.00

Series 46 - WWE Elite Collection (Mattel) 2016
Booker T - WWE Elite Collection (Mattel): $50.00+
Stevie Ray - WWE Elite Collection (Mattel): $30.00
Finn Balor - WWE Elite Collection (Mattel): $40.00
John Cena - WWE Elite Collection (Mattel): $30.00
Rusev - WWE Elite Collection (Mattel): $30.00
Sheamus - WWE Elite Collection (Mattel): $20.00

Series 47 A - WWE Elite Collection (Mattel) 2017
Aj Styles - WWE Elite Collection (Mattel): $25.00
Asuka - WWE Elite Collection (Mattel): $25.00
Big Boss Man - WWE Elite Collection (Mattel): $35.00
Cesaro - WWE Elite Collection (Mattel): $30.00
Kevin Owens - WWE Elite Collection (Mattel): $30.00
Tatanka - WWE Elite Collection (Mattel): $30.00

Series 47B - WWE Elite Collection (Mattel) 2017
Brian Pillman - WWE Elite Collection (Mattel): $35.00
Golddust - WWE Elite Collection (Mattel): $30.00
Kane - WWE Elite Collection (Mattel): $30.00
Konnor - WWE Elite Collection (Mattel): $20.00
Viktor - WWE Elite Collection (Mattel): $20.00
Rock - WWE Elite Collection (Mattel): $35.00

Series 48 - WWE Elite Collection (Mattel) 2017
Boogeyman - WWE Elite Collection (Mattel): $25.00
Cactus Jack - WWE Elite Collection (Mattel): $45.00
Dean Ambrose - WWE Elite Collection (Mattel): $25.00
Dolph Ziglar - WWE Elite Collection (Mattel): $25.00
Erick Rowan - WWE Elite Collection (Mattel): $20.00
Kalisto - WWE Elite Collection (Mattel): $20.00

Series 49 - WWE Elite Collection (Mattel) 2017
Apollo Crews - WWE Elite Collection (Mattel): $20.00
Becky Linch - WWE Elite Collection (Mattel): $20.00
Big Cass - WWE Elite Collection (Mattel): $20.00
Brutus Beefcake - WWE Elite Collection (Mattel): $30.00

Series 50 - WWE Elite Collection (Mattel) 2017
Baron Corbin - WWE Elite Collection (Mattel): $20.00
John Cena — WWE Elite Collection (Mattel): $30.00
Ryno - WWE Elite Collection (Mattel): $25.00
Shane McMahon - WWE Elite Collection (Mattel): $35.00
Stephanie McMahon - WWE Elite Collection (Mattel): $35.00
Warlord - WWE Elite Collection (Mattel): $30.00

Series 51 - WWE Elite Collection (Mattel) 2017
AJ Styles - WWE Elite Collection (Mattel): $30.00
Berzerker - WWE Elite Collection (Mattel): $30.00
Mankind - WWE Elite Collection (Mattel): $35.00
Roman Reigns - WWE Elite Collection (Mattel): $30.00
Sami Zayn - WWE Elite Collection (Mattel): $35.00+
Scott Hall - WWE Elite Collection (Mattel): $35.00

Series 52 - WWE Elite Collection (Mattel) 2017
Brawn Strowman - WWE Elite Collection (Mattel): $25.00
D-Lo Brown - WWE Elite Collection (Mattel): $25.00
Ken Shamrock - WWE Elite Collection (Mattel): $25.00
Kofi Kingston - WWE Elite Collection (Mattel): $25.00
Seth Rollins - WWE Elite Collection (Mattel): $30.00
Xavier Woods - WWE Elite Collection (Mattel): $25.00

Series 53 - WWE Elite Collection (Mattel) 2017
Alexa Bliss - WWE Elite Collection (Mattel): $20.00
Big E - WWE Elite Collection (Mattel): $25.00
Chris Jerico - WWE Elite Collection (Mattel): $40.00
Heath Slater - WWE Elite Collection (Mattel): $20.00
Kevin Owens - WWE Elite Collection (Mattel): $20.00
Miz - WWE Elite Collection (Mattel): $25.00

Series 54 - WWE Elite Collection (Mattel) 2017
Bray Wyatt - WWE Elite Collection (Mattel): $30.00
Charolette flair - WWE Elite Collection (Mattel): $30.00
Jey Uso - WWE Elite Collection (Mattel): $20.00
Jimmy Uso - WWE Elite Collection (Mattel): $20.00
John Cena - WWE Elite Collection (Mattel): $30.00
Rich Swan - WWE Elite Collection (Mattel): $20.00

Series 55 - WWE Elite Collection (Mattel) 2017
Big Cass - WWE Elite Collection (Mattel): $15.00
Brock Lesnar - WWE Elite Collection (Mattel): $40.00
Enzo Amore - WWE Elite Collection (Mattel): $15.00
James Ellsworth - WWE Elite Collection (Mattel): $15.00
Neville - WWE Elite Collection (Mattel): $25.00
Undertaker - WWE Elite Collection (Mattel): $35.00

Series 56 - WWE Elite Collection (Mattel) 2018
AJ Styles - WWE Elite Collection (Mattel): $30.00
Gentleman Jack Gallagher - WWE Elite Collection (Mattel): $20.00
Karl Anderson - WWE Elite Collection (Mattel): $20.00
Luke Gallows - WWE Elite Collection (Mattel): $20.00
Roman Reigns - WWE Elite Collection (Mattel): $25.00
Samoa Joe - WWE Elite Collection (Mattel): $20.00

Series 57 - WWE Elite Collection (Mattel) 2018

Barin Corbin - WWE Elite Collection (Mattel): $15.00
Jeff Hardy - WWE Elite Collection (Mattel): $20.00
Scotty 2 Hotty - WWE Elite Collection (Mattel): $15.00
Seth Rollins - WWE Elite Collection (Mattel): $25.00
Shinsuke Nakamura - WWE Elite Collection (Mattel): $25.00
Tye Dillinger - WWE Elite Collection (Mattel): $10.00

Series 58 - WWE Elite Collection (Mattel) 2018

Braun Strowman - WWE Elite Collection (Mattel): 25.00
Cesaro - WWE Elite Collection (Mattel): 25.00
Dean Ambrose - WWE Elite Collection (Mattel): 25.00
Matt Hardy - WWE Elite Collection (Mattel): 25.00
Mickie James - WWE Elite Collection (Mattel): 25.00+
Sheamus - WWE Elite Collection (Mattel): 25.00

Series 59 - WWE Elite Collection (Mattel) 2018

Chad Gable - WWE Elite Collection (Mattel): 25.00
Finn Balor - WWE Elite Collection (Mattel): 40.00+
Jason Jordan - WWE Elite Collection (Mattel): 25.00
Curt Angle - WWE Elite Collection (Mattel): 40.00
Miz - WWE Elite Collection (Mattel): 25.00
Zack Ryder - WWE Elite Collection (Mattel): 25.00

Series 60 - WWE Elite Collection (Mattel) 2018

Andre the Giant - WWE Elite Collection (Mattel): 50.00+
Elias - WWE Elite Collection (Mattel): 40.00
John Cena - WWE Elite Collection (Mattel): 25.00
Kofi Kingston - WWE Elite Collection (Mattel): 25.00
Triple H - WWE Elite Collection (Mattel): 25.00
Xavier Woods - WWE Elite Collection (Mattel): 25.00

Series 61 WWE Elite Collection (Mattel) 2018

Shane McMahon WWE Elite Collection: 25.00
AJ Styles WWE Elite Collection: 50.00+
Big E WWE Elite Collection: 30.00
Fandango WWE Elite Collection: 30.00
Tyler Breeze WWE Elite Collection: 30.00
Keven Owens WWE Elite Collection: 35.00+

Series 62 WWE Elite Collection (Mattel)

Akam WWE Elite Collection: 25.00
Braun Stowman WWE Elite Collection: 30.00
Dude Love WWE Elite Collection: 35.00
Rezar WWE Elite Collection: 30.00
Roman Reigns WWE Elite Collection: 30.00
Sting WWE Elite Collection: 35.00

Series 63 WWE Elite Collection (Mattel) 2019

Dean Ambrose WWE Elite Collection: 30.00
Dusty Rhodes WWE Elite Collection: 30.00
Kane WWE Elite Collection: 30.00
Sami Zayn WWE Elite Collection: 30.00
Shelton Benjamin WWE Elite Collection: 30.00
Shinsuke Nakamura WWE Elite Collection: 30.00

Series 64 WWE Elite Collection (Mattel)

Curt Hawkins WWE Elite Collection: 30.00
Jey Uso WWE Elite Collection: 30.00
Jimmy Uso WWE Elite Collection: 30.00
John Cena WWE Elite Collection: 30.00
Samoa Joe WWE Elite Collection`: 30.00
Seth Rollins WWE Elite Collection: 35.00+

Series 65 WWE Elite Collection (Mattel)

Aiden English WWE Elite Collection: 20.00
Eric Young WWE Elite Collection: 30.00+
Nia Jax WWE Elite Collection: 20.00
Roman Reigns WWE Elite Collection: 25.00
Ronda Rousey WWE Elite Collection: 30.00+
Resev WWE Elite Collection: 25.00

Best of Pay-Per-View 2014 WWE Elite Collection (Mattel)

Alberto Del Rio WWE Elite Collection: 30.00
C.M Punk WWE Elite Collection: 30.00
Curtis Axel WWE Elite Collection: 30.00
Jim Ross WWE Elite Collection: 30.00
Randy Orton WWE Elite Collection: 30.00

Exclusives WWE Elite Collection Mattel

Triple H (Wrestlemania 29) (Toys R Us) 2013: : 50.00
Triple H (DX Walgreens) 2005: : 50.00
Seth Rollins (Seth Cashes in) (Toys R Us) 2015: 50.00
Shawn Michaels (DX Walgreens) 2005: 50.00+
Samoa Joes (NXT Champion Walgreens) 2017: 50.00
Sasha Banks (Walgreens) 2017: 50.00
Mankind (Amazon) 2014: 50.00
Rocky Maivia Flasback (Target) 2014: 75.00
Jonn Cena Flashback (Toys R Us) 2015: 75.00
Kurt Angle Shield (Ringside) 2017: 50.00
Brock Lesnar WWE 2K17 (Walgreens) 2016: 75.00+
Chris Jericho the List (Walgreens) 2017: 50.00
Andre the Giant Flashback (Amazon) 2017: 75.00+
Brock Lesnar 21-1 (Toys R Us) 75.00+
Virgil: 75.00+

WWE Network Spotlight WWE Elite Collection 2015

AJ Styles WWE Elite Collection Network Spotlight (Wrestlemania 33): 40.00

Bayley WWE Elite Collection Network Spotlight (takover Broklyn): 20.00

Big Boss Man WWE Elite Collection Network Spotlight: 30.00

Dean Ambrose WWE Elite Collection Network Spotlight: 20.00

Finn Baylor WWE Elite Collection Network Spotlight: 40.00+

Hunter Hurst Helmsley WWE Elite Collection Network Spotlight: 20.00

Mr McMahon WWE Elite Collection Network Spotlight: 20.00

Ring Master Steve Austin WWE Elite Collection Network Spotlight: 30.00

Roman Reigns WWE Elite Collection Network Spotlight: 20.00

Shawn Michaels WWE Elite Collection Network Spotlight: 40.00

Undertaker WWE Elite Collection Network Spotlight: 40.00

Best of Attitude Era WWE Elite Collection 2018

Chris Jericho Best of Attitude Era WWE Elite Collection: 50.00+

Stone Cold Steve Austin Best of Attitude Era WWE Elite Collection: 40.00

The Rock Best of Attitude Era WWE Elite Collection: 40.00

Triple H Best of Attitude Era WWE Elite Collection: 40.00

Flashback WWE Elite Collection 2015

Virgil Flashback WWE Elite Collection: 75.00+

Hall of Champions WWE Elite Collection 2018

Batista WWE Elite Collection: 30.00

Dean Ambrose Vs The Miz (Battle Pack) WWE Elite Collection: 25.00

Eddie Guerrero WWE Elite Collection: 70.00+

John Cena Vs Batista (Battle Pack) WWE Elite Collection: 20.00

Rakishi WWE Elite Collection: 20.00

Road Dog WWE Elite Collection: 20.00

Undertaker WWE Elite Collection: 30.00

Ron Simmons WWE Elite Collection: 65.00+

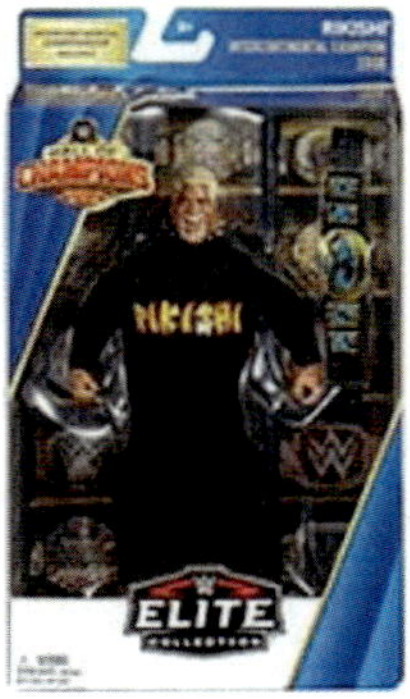

NXT Series 1 WWE Elite Collection 2018

Austin Aries NXT WWE Elite Collection: 20.00

Bayley NXT WWE Elite Collection: 20.00

No Way Jose NXT WWE Elite Collection: 20.00

Seth Rollins NXT WWE Elite Collection: 25.00

NXT Series 2 WWE Elite Collection 2017

Asuka NXT WWE Elite Collection: 40.00

Dash Wilder NXT WWE Elite Collection: 15.00

Scott Dawson NXT WWE Elite Collection: 15.00

Shinsuke Nakamura NXT WWE Elite Collection: 25.00

NXT Series 3 WWE Elite Collection 2018

Alexander Rusev NXT WWE Elite Collection: 25.00

Bobby Roode NXT WWE Elite Collection: 20.00

Ember Moon NXT WWE Elite Collection: 20.00

Roman Reigns NXT WWE Elite Collection: 25.00

PPV Wrestlemania XXX WWE Elite Collection 2014

Bray Wyatt PPV Wrestlemania XXX WWE Elite Collection: 20.00:

Daniel Bryan PPV Wrestlemania XXX WWE Elite Collection: 20.00

John Cena PPV Wrestlemania XXX WWE Elite Collection: 20.00

Kane Corporate Suite PPV Wrestlemania XXX WWE Elite Collection: 30.00

Undertaker PPV Wrestlemania XXX WWE Elite Collection: 25.00

Summer Slam WWE Elite Collection

Dean Ambrose Summer Slam WWE Elite Collection 2018: 20.00

Edge Summer Slam WWE Elite Collection 2018: 30.00

Finn Balor Summer Slam WWE Elite Collection 2017: 30.00

Mankind Summer Slam WWE Elite Collection 2017: 25.00

Mat Hardy Summer Slam WWE Elite Collection 2018: 25.00

Seth Rollins Summer Slam WWE Elite Collection 2018: 35.00

Then Now Forever Series 1 WWE Elite Collection 2016

Bam Bam Bigelow Then Now Forever WWE Elite Collection: : 40.00:

Rock Then Now Forever WWE Elite Collection: 25.00

Rusev Then Now Forever WWE Elite Collection: 25.00

Tyler Breeze Then Now Forever WWE Elite Collection: 20.00

Then Now Forever Series 2 WWE Elite Collection 2017

Earthquake Then Now Forever WWE Elite Collection: 30.00

Macho Man Randy Savage Then Now Forever WWE Elite Collection: 40.00

Sami Zayn Then Now Forever WWE Elite Collection: 30.00

Typhoon Then Now Forever WWE Elite Collection: 30.00

Then Now Forever Series 3 WWE Elite Collection 2017

Chad Gable Then Now Forever WWE Elite Collection: 20.00

Jason Jordan Then Now Forever WWE Elite Collection: 20.00:

Miss Elizabeth Then Now Forever WWE Elite Collection: 50.00

Seth Rollins Then Now Forever WWE Elite Collection: 25.00

WWE All-Stars WWE Elite Collection 2011

Jake Roberts vs Randy Orton All-Stars WWE Elite Collection: 100.00:

Macho Man Randy Savage vs John Morrison All-Stars WWE Elite Collection: 100.00

Stone Cold Steve Austin vs C.M Punk All-Stars WWE Elite Collection: 150.00

Wrestlemania 30 - WWE Elite Collection (Mattel) 2011

Bret Hitman Hart WWE Elite Collection - Wrestlemania 30: $75.00+

Shawn Michaels (Hairy Stomach) - Wrestlemania 30: $50.00

Shawn Michaels (Bare Stomach) WWE - Wrestlemania 30: $50.00

Wrestlemania 31 - WWE Elite Collection (Mattel) 2015

Kane WWE Elite Collection - Wrestlemania 31: $50.00+

UndertakerWWE Elite Collection - Wrestlemania 31: $50.00+

Made in the USA
San Bernardino, CA
25 July 2020

76050437R00093